GREATLY, DEEPLY

Ben Morrell
with Lisa Morrell

GREATLY, DEEPLY

AEON ENTERPRISES, INC. OCTOBER 2013

AeonEnt.com

Cover illustration by
Beth Morrell

Book Design by
Aeon Enterprises, Inc.

ISBN- 978-0-9886275-7-4

V1.0_r1

Produced and Printed in the U.S.A.

ACKNOWLEDGMENTS

A month before Ben died, he gathered together a team of amazing volunteers to help him publish a book about his cancer journey. These friends really made things happen.

Erika Mitchell, who selected most of the blog entries in this book, edited, shepherded us all along, and held my hand during the difficult parts

Rowena Portch, for her expert formatting and layout prowess, and her help and advice in the publishing process

Katie Ferguson, for her extensive, sharp-eyed and sequential editing, and taking on much of the boring copying/pasting

Marie Morache, for selecting one year of blog entries and reviewing the other selections with a great deal of heart

Matthew Murakami, for getting things off to a great start with help coordinating and brainstorming

Nathan Fenno, for writing the riveting back-cover copy and his insightful book-structure commentary

Greg Osborne, who poured himself out in writing the book's Introduction

Cheryl Gilbert, for proof-reading and making sure all quotes were correct and cited

Lexi Forrest, for her helpful feedback as a beta reader

Beth Morrell, for painting "Deep Roots" to help raise money for Ben's treatments and then later re-imagining and designing it in book cover form

Jenifer Morrell, who collaborated on the prologue material as an expert on Ben's overall life story

Everyone who abundantly loved and prayed for Ben

God, the Author of our paths and Creator of stories

Seeing Ben's work in print and out into the world makes my heart happy. Thank you all. Ben would have been thrilled to see us complete this project.

—Lisa Morrell

Forward

BENJAMIN MICHAEL MORRELL WAS BORN to Paul and Jenifer Morrell in Long Beach, California in 1982. Soon, he was joined by siblings Adam and Beth. The Morrells moved to Bothell, Washington in 1991, and started attending Crossroads Bible Church. Growing up, Ben enjoyed playing in the backyard woods, as well as putting on plays for his family. His love of technology was fostered by his dad. He quietly observed his mom cooking and became an excellent chef later in life. Ben's loyalty and commitment contributed to friendships that lasted the rest of his life.

At King's High School in Seattle, Ben wrote for the school newspaper and joined the drama program, King's Players. His passion for missions grew as he had the opportunity to travel on various mission trips to Slovakia, Italy, Russia and Spain with his school and church.

Ben attended Bellevue Community College while working at Barnes and Noble. At that time, he started his blog, 802Heaven, where he developed his writing and indulged his sense of humor. He continued on to Seattle Pacific University, graduating in 2006 with a degree in computer networking. He became IT Manager of Taproot Theatre that same year.

In 2005, Ben married Lisa Massingill. Less than two years later, Ben was diagnosed with a soft tissue sarcoma, DSRCT. His doctor gave him a 17% chance of surviving five years.

He astounded the medical community by living six years.

In the last few weeks of his life, Ben enjoyed spending time with family and friends in Bellevue, WA. He was called home to be with his Lord on May 9, 2013.

What follows are blog posts from the years of his cancer treatments. These posts were selected because we felt they told the story of how cancer deepened the value of Ben's faith. Full archives can be found online at www.802heaven.com.

—Jenifer Morrell and Lisa Morrell

Introduction

"Father, if You are willing, remove this cup from Me; yet not My will, but Yours be done."

— Luke 22:42 NASB

JESUS PRAYED THIS PRAYER SHORTLY before His crucifixion. The suffering He was called to was not something He anticipated with joy, but He was willing to endure it for the glory of God. His strength in the face of tremendous suffering has given Christians all over the world hope that their suffering is not in vain. As such, Jesus's prayer in Gethsemane has been echoed by suffering saints for as long as the church has existed.

Ben Morrell was one of those saints. Instead of giving in to fear, anger, or bitterness, he sought to glorify God with everything he did. He strove to discern what God's purpose for his suffering was, and continued his arduous journey to the end of his days bearing fruits of the Holy Spirit: love, joy, peace, patience, kindness, goodness, faithfulness, gentleness, and self-control.

Ben was called to suffer a rare type of cancer called Desmoplastic Small Round Cell Tumors (DSRCT). His courage in handling this gave many people hope, but it did not define his life.

Ben did not immediately make a strong impression on people. A natural introvert, he gradually opened up to people as he grew more comfortable around them. Those who entered Ben's circle of trust experienced his Christ-like love for others. Ben naturally encouraged people. He was open about his own struggles, and he took other people's struggles to heart. He was easy to confide in since he empathetically offered his thoughts without judgment or pretension. Even though his fatal illness typically dwarfed other's problems, he didn't treat them as though their struggles were inconsequential. He encouraged people to send him prayer requests at the end of many of his blog posts, and he prayed for them while he waited to see doctors at MD Anderson.

His blog was read by hundreds of friends and family members, and even people searching for information about DSRCT who he never met in person. They looked at 802heaven.com often, because they were attracted to his faith, his attitude, his gift with words, his message of hope, his encouragement, and his honesty.

Though writing was his favorite form of

expression, he created art through multiple mediums. He was very good at envisioning what he wanted to create, and making his vision become a reality. He enjoyed recreating images from his mind on paper using paints and pencils. He used cooking to bless the people he cared about; the Food Network was typically his channel of choice in hospitals.

Naturally proficient with technology, he was always at the forefront of technological trends. He enthusiastically offered tech support to his friends for all their computing needs. He once tweeted, "Friends don't let friends take their computers to #GeekSquad."

Ben's love for technology, combined with his love for missions, led him to employment at OC International. As the IT director, he implemented the tools the organization needed to encourage communication. He dreamed about the future and the possibilities technology would unlock. As he wrote to his supervisor at OC International days before he died, "I know that God has provided me with an imagination and an ability to plan for what the future might look like." He shared his vision of future communication tools to spread the gospel with his supervisor days before his death. His supervisor had this to say: "The face of world missions will never be the same because of that conversation."

Like most of us, Ben struggled to identify God's purpose for his life. He endured intense levels of suffering that limited his activity, but refused to concede to cancer. He continued to serve God through his job at OC International, and never stopped petitioning God to heal his body, even during his final hours.

As time moves on and his friends and family join him in Heaven, Ben's message will remain on Earth. Just as his story reached a new audience when people posted on social networks with messages of grief in the hours after his passing, it will continue to reach far beyond his circles of acquaintance for years to come as people hear about this book from people who enjoy it. What they'll find when they open these pages are the words of a kindred soul, honestly written by a man who bravely chose to bare his struggles so others could benefit from his journey.

Ben is not here on Earth today, but his writings are an invitation for you to partake in the love, joy, and peace his life proclaimed through his faith in Jesus Christ. I hope this book encourages and challenges you in the same way his friendship encouraged and challenged me.

— Greg Osborne

2007

MAY, SEATTLE

THURSDAY, MAY 3, 2007

Abnormal Abdominal

I **SPENT ABOUT 6 HOURS YESTERDAY** in the lower recesses of the Primary Eastside Care Clinic while I had a number of tests run on me. Some of you have been aware that a week and a half ago I was having some strange pains in my abdominal region and spent a couple of days at the doctor's office waiting for blood work, etc. They scheduled an abdominal ultrasound a week and a half ago and yesterday was that day.

I got to the place about 7:30am and by 8:30am I had had the ultrasound and the Doctor had looked at them and said he wanted to do a CT (cat?) scan. Insert a couple hours of waiting and drinking strange materials and an IV and some radioactive compound and they sent me home.

Last evening about 6 I got a call from the doctor and he said that the CT scans showed that I had some abdominal abnormalities and the next step is to do some surgery so that the doctors can look at the several abnormal growths I have.

I'm not going to lie to you, I'm scared about what this could be.

Surgery Tomorrow

BIOPSY TOMORROW MORNING/ AFTERNOON. They are going to go in there and get a little bit of whatever it is that is plaguing my insides.

I'll be going into the hospital after I'm done with the cancer expert and then the biopsy. I'm not nervous so much for the biopsy being as I will be asleep, I am a little nervous about the results (3 to 5 days later). It's hard. It's like my normal mind is either not able to grasp I have cancer or it is ok with it, and then sometimes my subconscious starts screaming in the background and I completely break down. So if you happen to be talking with me don't be surprised if I suddenly lose it and start crying. I'm nervous and it's stressful.

I know God is in control, it's just that I would like to learn a lesson from this and come out ok on the other end. I don't know if that is what God has in store for me, but I'm trying to be open to anything.

WEDNESDAY, MAY 9, 2007

Waiting

I WANTED TO LET YOU ALL KNOW that we're still waiting for a diagnosis. I covet all your prayers. Emotionally I'm pretty broken (cried at the end of Spiderman 3 on Saturday). It takes me about 2 hours in the mornings to make the nervousness go away (a lot of prayer, Bible readings and worship songs).

Not sure when I'll be able to get back to work. I think I've got it pretty fixed at the moment so beyond the occasional question nothing is breaking. So while they might miss me I don't think my absence is causing them problems (I hope).

THURSDAY, MAY 10, 2007

Friday

I HAVE A DOCTOR'S APPOINTMENT TOMORROW at 3pm. I was told by the doctor that he wouldn't see me again unless it was cancer.

FRIDAY, MAY 11, 2007

Diagnosis

I'M NOT GOING TO LIE TO YOU. When I imagined going into the doctor's office today I imagined hearing that it was going to be bad. I really am not creative enough to imagine how bad. I have a rare form of cancer called desmoplastic, which are small round cell tumors. This is an aggressive form of cancer that occurs in males in their teens to early 20s.

I'm starting aggressive chemotherapy on Tuesday. I'll be in the hospital 4 days and then home for about 2 weeks, then into the hospital again for 4 days, then home for another 2 weeks, and then back in the hospital again for 4 days.

I'm doing ok right now. I don't want to die. I want to live and fight this thing and look back at this 15 years from now and marvel at the goodness of God.

SATURDAY, MAY 12, 2007

Brokenness

"BLESSED BE THE LORD, WHO DAILY BEARS our burden, the God who is our Salvation."

—Psalm 68:10

There was a song that we used to sing in Jr High and High School that had the following lyrics: "Brokenness, Brokenness is what I long for. Brokenness is what I need. Brokenness is what you want from me..."

I was thinking about that this morning. I don't think I ever wanted to be "broken" by God. Or be at a place where I seriously wanted God to have to put me back together. I don't know that I am completely at that point now or not, but I'm really close to broken. God as we read in the Bible is the great healer. Jesus heals all sorts of people in the first years of his ministry (read the Gospel of John) and Jesus there is doing the work of God. So I know that even though I may be broken now, that God can heal me. And it won't be some sloppy glue job either. I'll be better than I was before.

I was explaining something to Lisa this morning about my state of mind: Sometimes I start thinking about everything, and then I just get shocked and panicked. At that point it's best for me to move to a place where I can cry. Most of the tears I have shed these past few days have been because I have been touched by someone reaching out to me or a concern for someone else. From tears I'm able to move into laughter and then things start to be better. These steps however are completely encompassed by prayer, scripture reading, and worshiping God through music. So if you are around me and I have a kind of dazed look on my face you might want to see if you can get me to cry (errrr, that didn't sound so good...).

I've also decided that (as the verse at the top

points to) I'm going to only focus on my life one day at a time. When I think ahead toward the future and everything I've got to go through I do not know how I will do it. God's grace is going to be there as are His Peace and His Strength, but I cannot control the future by worrying about it. I REALLY, REALLY need to focus on the here and now. One day at a time.

SUNDAY, MAY 13, 2007

Prayer Meeting last night

LAST NIGHT LISA AND I INVITED a bunch of people over to her parents' house (it was kind of an "all call" via email) to pray with me/ for me. I didn't get a final count of how many people were there but it was up into the 30's. Friends and family and friends of family that I didn't really know. There was prayer, there was singing, and there were Bible verses read. I felt the peace of God descend on me in a wonderful way. I was able to sleep very well last night (without any kind of medication).

MONDAY, MAY 14, 2007

Setting the house in order

I START CHEMOTHERAPY TOMORROW. I don't know many details at this time. I've been doing stuff today to save us some money and make Lisa's life a little easier if I can't help out.

I also met with my friend Dan briefly at Starbucks today and we talked for a bit. The things he had to say were kind of hard to hear. When I got home I sat down and talked with God about them. The things I got from the conversation as well as my time with God afterwards were as follows:

Christ gave his life for me on the cross ~2000 years ago. By becoming a Christian I gave my life to God to do with as He wanted. This is God's free gift to human kind that we are saved from eternal death (Hell) because of Christ's sacrifice for us those many years ago. In exchange we get to go to heaven for believing in God/ Jesus.

The difficult part of this is that God can, and will, call us to do whatever it is He wants us to do to glorify His name on earth. God has my life, and as my friend pointed out, God has called me out of the mundane-ness of a normal life and has asked me for more. I don't know if that ultimately means that this test will be the end of my life (it's God's to take) or if I'll have many more years and lots more tests and trials. I don't know that I'll ever stop praying for God to heal me, but above all else my life is His and I want to do with it what He wants me to do with it.

I was also reminded that the Bible says that God has ordained all of our days. He knew us from before we were born to our very last breath. I don't know the outcome of my life until it's over. But God has ordained it, every day I am God's.

I will not polish this over for you. Being completely in God's control and not being able to do anything yourself is scary. But He also provides a peace and a strength that comes from giving my life to Him and letting Him control what happens.

Always, forever, for God's Glory.

This morning between services at church the elders and a couple of pastors gathered around Lisa and I, anointed us with oil, and prayed over us. It was a very powerful time of prayer with a lot of Godly men that I know and look up to. My prayer is that one day I would be one of those men praying fervently over someone else who needs it.

I wanted to thank the person who left the comment in my previous entry about the community of people that have what I have, and thank them for the offer to join the community. At this point in the game, however, I don't know that I can handle too much information about this right now. Important things that will keep me healthy are important to me to know, but I don't want to know odds (God works no matter what the odds) or hear stories about people that haven't made it.

Ben was admitted to the hospital for his first chemotherapy treatment from May 15th – May 19th, 2007. After those days of continuous chemotherapy infusion, he came home to rest.

SATURDAY, MAY 19, 2007

Post chemo breakdown

AT THE MOMENT I FEEL A LITTLE light headed, but I have been eating and taking meds has been happening. Later this week I'm going to get the PICC line in my arm removed and have a port put into my chest so they can do all sorts of things like draw blood or put chemo in me.

I'm a little tired I think now. I plan to post more as I have energy and things to talk about.

To God be the Glory, forever, amen.

SUNDAY, MAY 20, 2007

Amazing Grace

I WISH PEOPLE WERE AT CHURCH all the time. Then I could go and hang out there and worship God and pray with people all the time. Sundays are great for this but sadly enough today I didn't have very much energy. Lisa and I went to church but we only went to one service and I had to beat a hasty retreat because I was feeling light headed.

In other news my body has started to lie to me a little more. Last night I spent more than a couple hours in the bathroom because my body kept saying that I really needed to go (I didn't). Also I don't feel hungry, but I know I need to eat. I have minor pains that flash through my body and whatnot that I don't pay much mind.

The times they are a chang'n

I AM STRUGGLING RIGHT NOW with all the changes that are going on in my life. All of them are things that I have caused but don't have any effect over. Today the wonderful person who will be taking care of Niko long term swung by and picked him up. I think that hit me harder than almost anything that has changed so far. Granted we haven't had that little bird very long and he'll be living at the church, but it's just another change.

Lisa has told me that the changes are all ok and that they are going to be good. God has blessed us with so many people who are willing to help us sometimes it just makes me want to cry.

This isn't easy. I feel like I'm going to need this all to let up at some point. Yes God is my rock and my shelter, but how long is this storm going to last? I feel like it's probably just blowing in.

MONDAY, MAY 21, 2007

Understanding David

THIS MORNING WAS THE CLOSEST morning thus far I have felt to "sick" (I'm not sure if that is due to chemicals in my system or an increased metabolism that wants me to keep shoveling food into my system even though I don't feel like it). Lisa got out of bed and made me a fruit smoothie which helped how I was feeling greatly. She then did her morning things and studied her Bible. As she was leaving for the day she suggested I read over Psalm 119.

Psalm 119, besides being the longest Psalm in the Bible, is not unknown to me. My small group Bible study spent a good 3 to 5 months studying it. I listened to it twice this morning via BibleGateway.com.

During our study I think we took possibly a too "spiritual" look at the chapter. David, or whoever the author was, continually cries out for salvation. I seem to remember we talked about the author wanting spiritual salvation, relying on the promise of God for a savior to Israel. I however think that the cry of the author of Psalm 119 was salvation from death. David wanted to be rescued from the people and things that persecuted him so he could continue the Lord's work just as much as he hoped for the salvation of Israel through a Messiah.

Psalm 119 cries out for delivery from evil so

that the author may continue to be God's agent in the world.

God has brought me this far in life, he's given me a wonderful wife, a great education, blessed me with all sorts of wonderful skills and abilities... I want to survive this to see what, or where, God will have for me next. However the point of my life is God's glory, not my own. I want God's glory the most, however it comes (it's taken me a week, possibly two, to be able to say that and mean it fully).

TUESDAY, MAY 22, 2007

Prayer for the morning

NIGHT-TIMES AREN'T MY BEST times. Because of this I sometimes wish I could sleep through the day and stay awake at night to deal with the strangeness's that my body chooses to become at night (the problem with that is I wouldn't get to see anyone!).

This morning was the first time I actually got sick since chemo started. The strange part about it is that other from the cleanup that had to follow I think it was better for me than worse. Last Thursday when I had hiccups I burned something in my throat with the acid reflux and it has made swallowing water painful. Since getting sick this morning that is no longer a problem. (Praise God!) I also wasn't feeling like eating much but I've been snacking away since about 8am this morning. Blessings from the strangest places.

THURSDAY, MAY 24, 2007

Overly familiar with the E-room

-by Lisa-

WELL, BEN HASN'T BEEN POSTING lately because he's too sick. Yesterday we had to take a trip to the emergency room for a few hours, and came back with Ben still feeling awful, but with more drugs to take. Today his mom stayed with him at home, and he ended up needing to go to the emergency room again-- he couldn't take any of the antibiotics they gave us. He's going to be spending the night at Overlake Hospital. The danger is that his white blood cell count is so low that he won't be able to fight off infections and sickness.

I think we're both discouraged and definitely at a loss for what to do. This is only a few days after the first round of chemo, for goodness sakes! We can only pray that this is the low point, and remember that although we are completely out of control, God is in control! In fact, I guess we've always been completely out of control our whole lives, it just doesn't feel like it a lot. Me not being able to help Ben right now just "brings that home."

TUESDAY, MAY 29, 2007

Hunger on the rise... mindgames

THIS MORNING I WAS ABLE to get up, make myself a bowl of oatmeal and eat most of it (as well as some apple juice). This is the most I have eaten at one time in a while. It no longer hurts as much as it used to, and I'll be diving into lunch here in a bit. Continue to pray my hunger will increase and that I'll be able to gain and keep some weight on this week.

In other news it's kind of hard feeling better now. Lisa and I are planning on going on a little mini-vacation this weekend and then after that the Chemo starts again, and then my feeling well will take a dive again. Honestly it's hard, really hard, to think that I'm going to go in for treatment next Tuesday and then have to go through this cycle again. I am praying that next time around it'll be a little easier and I'll have a better idea about how to take care of my body.

JUNE, SEATTLE

FRIDAY, JUNE 1, 2007

Doctor's visit and an Island

THIS MORNING I MET WITH my cancer doctor and we talked about what they are going to do next time to keep the sickness levels down. He said though that on top of everything that I am on a very heavy chemo treatment and being sick could very well just be part of the treatment (I'm in a 72 hour straight chemo, most stuff I've seen documented says that chemo treatments are a couple of hours. A "day trip" to the hospital type thing).

It was really hard seeing the doctor this morning as the last time I saw him he laid all sorts of bad news on me. I couldn't help but think he was going to hit me with something else this time. Not the case however.

TUESDAY, JUNE 5, 2007

Where the nurse knows your name

Today was a very typical first day of chemo. This past weekend I was able to purchase an MP3 player that allows me to listen to and download unlimited amounts of music from Rhapsody. I was able to make use of this this morning as I laid in bed for a couple hours listening to some of the music I had queued up. It's a great comfort to have access to worship songs when I want them, without having to rely on the radio.

The catheter in my chest continues to be slightly strange. Last night I mentioned to one of the doctors that it was a little sore (like a "2" or "3" on the pain scale) and the doctor instantly wanted to know if I wanted any Vicodin. I thought that was a little heavy-handed, so I declined. But I was informed that when you're on the 15th floor-- the cancer ward-- that you have access to almost whatever drugs you want. I'm sure if I was more into swallowing pills, this would excite me. As it is, the thought of having to swallow more pills for just slight pain seems ridiculous.

Daytime television. What can I say? So many channels, so little to watch. So I pretty much give up watching. I do a lap every couple hours, see if I'm missing anything, and keep going. I have, however, been taking in the Mariners games. It's kinda a newfound sickness/hobby. And I hope as soon as I'm well enough, to get to at least one game.

TUESDAY, JUNE 12, 2007

Light? End? Tunnel?

IT'S REALLY HARD TO SIT here on the couch and feel horrible (headache, queasy, bathroom trips every 30 minutes - 1 hour, hard to eat, etc.) and know that next week, odds are very good that I will be feeling at the peak of health again. I just have to get through the rest of this week with my obliterated health first. Needless to say I think I'm a little discouraged about feeling so ill right now. Everyone has been great and the support has been almost unlimited, but I still feel bad. I don't want to sound like I am complaining, I guess I just need prayer for endurance and strength. Badly.

Often after his rounds of chemotherapy, Ben's white blood cell count would dip to the point that his immune system was ineffective. The first sign of infection was usually a fever. During those times he'd be admitted to the hospital for antibiotics and monitoring. In mid-June, Ben also contracted "thrush" – a painful mouth infection which is a side-effect of chemo.

TUESDAY, JUNE 19, 2007

He knows

I'VE BEEN HAVING SOME PRETTY crazy and vivid dreams these past couple of days. Some of them are strange, others are touching, and some just leave me confused. I had one dream last night where I was fighting in a battle against all sorts of horrific fantasy type creatures. I was adorned in a glowing white armour and was fighting with two swords. My close friends were also on the battlefield and were wearing different types of armour and fighting with different types of weapons, but we were all out there fighting. We were all doing really well and the battle turned in our favor and the creatures fled.

We all returned to our camp (tents, pavilions, etc.) to celebrate the victory, and while we were reclining and kicking back a character came to me. I remember that he was dressed very nicely and there was a beautiful woman with him. I don't remember much more than that other than in my dream I knew who he was. I was afraid of him and moved around the camp to try to avoid him. In my dream this character was the Devil. I finally ended up in a tent with a couple of my best friends. Then the devil came in and sat down next to me. I can't recall what he said to me but part of what happened in my dream was that he cheapened my armour and my swords. What had been metal before now appeared to me to be simple plastic. At this point my best friend stood up and rebuked the devil and we left the tent. After that I wasn't followed anymore and I was able to celebrate with my friends and family without fear of being followed.

I don't know really why I shared the above with you, but it's kind of an example of the dreams I've been having.

This morning I spent some time in the book of Mark. Jesus really spends a lot of time healing in that book. This was again a reminder to me that Jesus IS the great healer and when He heals He heals completely and He heals well. I love that about the Lord, when He does something He does it greatly. He doesn't do it 25% of the way or 63% of the way He does it 100%. Now of course from our view sometimes things look a little off, but really our Lord does what is not only good for us, but what is GREAT. He knows when my throat needs to heal, how to heal it and what I need most for His glory. He knows if making it to my brother's wedding is good for me and/or the place I need to be. He knows and He cares.

Something that I really enjoy doing is looking back and seeing, with hindsight, how God has taken care of me and watched over me. The parts and pieces that didn't make sense at the time that make sense now. One example is how this whole thing started: I had a strange pain in my lower back and abdomen so I went to the doctor. He examined me and proclaimed it was constipation but just because he wanted to have an abdominal ultrasound done. Well, that led to finding the cancer. The "funny" thing is that I've never had that pain again since they've found the cancer. God is watching out for me.

In tongue news it doesn't burn this morning. It feels like I have scabs on the back of my tongue. I am going to avoid solid foods today in hopes that I don't do damage to something that is probably healing. It's been a week now since I've eaten a meal of solid foods. It's tough. God knows how much I enjoy food and there has to be a lesson in this I'm just trying to figure it out. Either way, He knows what I need.

On June 25th, Ben had a CT scan to check to see how the chemotherapy was affecting his tumors. He had to wait until the next day for the results.

TUESDAY, JUNE 26, 2007

Morning Prayer

DEAR LORD,

I AM AFRAID THIS MORNING. I fear the news that the doctor will bring me. Lord I need your strength today to face this. I need your peace Father as well, calm my heart and mind as the time approaches. Father, no matter what the outcome of this test help me to praise your name. I am nervous and you are the only one that can grant me peace. Lord, I want to be healed, to tell the world of your healing power. You know what is best though Father and You know how best to go about doing it. My heart and soul are heavy with this trial, please Lord provide me some good news.

Thank you Lord for your faithfulness and the blessings in my life. Thank you for friends and family and everyone who is praying for me. Be glorified today Lord.

Amen

Good news and a bit of a surprise

WELL LADIES AND GENTLEMEN, I have been to the doctor and am home again.

After the 2nd round of chemo my tumors have shrunk. All of them have diminished in size, some drastically and some only slightly. When Lisa looked at the scans she could tell they had shrunk so it's not just medical, "These are smaller... really" type thing. PRAISE THE LORD. That was what we have been praying for. It is super encouraging to know that the chemo has been working, that the stuff I have been going through has actually had an effect.

After that news there was a bit of a surprise

as well. It appears that I am to undergo 7 rounds of chemo. Not just 3. (He had originally said 3 and then surgery, so Lisa, Nancy {Lisa's mom} and I were a little surprised to hear I'd be undergoing 7 rounds.) Rounds 4, 5 and 7 will be longer (5 days) but fewer drugs (2 instead of 3) and we're still trying to figure out the best way to head off the thrush after chemo so I can eat. So, it looks like we're still a ways out from surgery (3 to 4 months?) but God is good.

WEDNESDAY, JUNE 27, 2007

Round and Round we go

IT'S STRANGE, THIS MORNING I am nervous. This will be the start of my 3rd chemo and I know more of what to expect and how to handle it than I did my past two visits to Virginia Mason. I think I am probably nervous about starting to feel sick again. I like feeling well and not having to take medication to feel that way.

I find myself thinking about the news I got yesterday a lot. I find a lot of hope in the news that the chemo is working. I find hope in the fact that God has chosen to work through those drugs and to diminish the cancer in my body. He is good and worthy of our praise!

JULY, SEATTLE

MONDAY, JULY 2, 2007

Strange hair and pant sizes

HERE IT IS MONDAY MORNING, day 2, after chemo round 3. I'm really not sure what this week has in store for me... but then again I honestly never do. Lisa suggested earlier this week that I write my brother a letter/ toast in case I couldn't make it to the wedding this weekend.

The contents of said letter had crossed my mind a time or two since then but last night at about 1am when I got up to go to the bathroom the contents of that letter hit me like a ton of bricks. I had to pull out my laptop and write the whole letter last night because I had that feeling that I either 1) Would lie awake for hours thinking about it if I didn't write it or 2) Would forget everything I felt was going to be so good to say in the morning.

On the flip side however I feel that it's a really good letter and honestly what is one of my major activities during the day anyway? That's right sleeping. What's a couple hours in the AM for a couple hours in the later AM or PM? Ya gotta strike while the iron is hot I guess (or when the brain is working).

TUESDAY, JULY 3, 2007

Death and Life

PSALM 91, NIV

1 Whoever dwells in the shelter of the Most High will rest in the shadow of the Almighty.[a]

2 I will say of the Lord, "He is my refuge and my fortress, my God, in whom I trust."

3 Surely he will save you from the fowler's snare and from the deadly pestilence.

4 He will cover you with his feathers, and under his wings you will find refuge; his faithfulness will be your shield and rampart.

5 You will not fear the terror of night, nor the arrow that flies by day,

6 nor the pestilence that stalks in the darkness, nor the plague that destroys at midday.

7 A thousand may fall at your side, ten thousand at your right hand, but it will not come near you.

8 You will only observe with your eyes and see

the punishment of the wicked.

9 If you say, "The Lord is my refuge," and you make the Most High your dwelling,

10 no harm will overtake you, no disaster will come near your tent.

11 For he will command his angels concerning you to guard you in all your ways;

12 they will lift you up in their hands, so that you will not strike your foot against a stone.

13 You will tread on the lion and the cobra; you will trample the great lion and the serpent.

14 "Because he[b] loves me," says the Lord, "I will rescue him; I will protect him, for he acknowledges my name.

15 He will call on me, and I will answer him; I will be with him in trouble, I will deliver him and honor him.

16 With long life I will satisfy him and show him my salvation."

When I was first diagnosed with the cancer I have I kept thinking about how I was carrying around the method for my own death in my abdomen. Untreated the tumors in my body would kill me. It was like a time bomb. Granted no one knows how much time they've got on the earth, but my odds were FAR, FAR better of getting hit by a vehicle of some type than getting this type of cancer.

Early this morning (again with the AM thinking) I was thinking over it again and God talked to me about it. While I am carrying death in my body, I carry eternal life in my heart. God gave His son, Jesus, to die for me on the cross to forgive my sins. So while things in my physical body are heading south and can kill me, there is safety in the spiritual. There is life there; life that cannot be denied by a tumor in my gut.

God also has brought a couple of instances these past 12 hours into my life to lead me to a Bible verse. Psalm 91. I've encountered it in several places now and I think God is trying to tell me something. I don't know the end result of this chemo and cancer, and I don't want to read into things, but Psalm 91 is at least saying that my trust should be the Lord, and that is where I will find my protection. Thus, I will continue to trust in my savior and see what he has in store for my life!

WEDNESDAY, JULY 4, 2007

An evening prayer request

MY WHITE BLOOD CELL COUNT today was at 5600 (4k to 10k is the "good" range). My platelets however were pretty low, so I don't know if that means my white cells will be coming down in the next few days or not.

I get blood drawn again on Friday and will be discussing with my nurse if going to Ellensburg for my brother's wedding would be a good move or not (probably by then I would have crashed or not as Friday about 2pm is officially "Crash Time"). We'll see though.

THURSDAY, JULY 5, 2007

bleh

I FEEL BAD. THIS COULD VERY WELL be the lowest energy level I have felt to date with chemo. I haven't eaten anything today because I don't have the energy, I've barely drank anything, and generally I spend the day on the couch I'm considering going back to bed.

I almost wish I would crash just so that I could go into the hospital and start feeling better (all the wonderful things they can put through my IV). I'm tired, I feel lame.

They tell me round 4 and 5 of chemo will be a little lighter than 1-3... that would be nice. I wish I could cook. I miss having the energy to cook. I think maybe that is why I spend so much time watching the Food Network. It's a hope for me. Anyway, I can't type anymore.

After this round of chemotherapy, Ben's white blood cell count plummeted, a condition called "neutropenia." He was admitted to the hospital to be given drugs and monitored. The day of his brother's wedding, Ben was in the hospital but was able to watch the ceremony via webcam.

SATURDAY JULY 7, 2007

Letter to Adam

DEAR ADAM,

I'd like to apologize right off the bat for not being able to be there this weekend. Having cancer and the complications that go with it wasn't part of my plan when I envisioned being involved in your wedding... That and you didn't have some excuse like that 2 years ago when I got married. As I am most likely either in the hospital or too sick at the moment to get to where you are, I wanted to take a moment to write to you and convey some things that 2 years of marriage have taught me, your older brother.

First off, remarkably, stems directly from why I can't be there with you this weekend. While I NEVER hope you have to endure anything like this in your life, I sincerely hope that you will get to experience a positive side effect that it has brought on. I could NOT have gotten as far as I have today without the help of my very supportive and loving wife Lisa. I pray that you and Shelly will be able to experience the kind of bond of support that Lisa and I have experienced sometime in your marriage. I don't know if that can happen without hardship, and I know it sounds horrible wishing something like that for you so close to your wedding, but that is the glue of marriage. Cling first to God and then to each other when the hard times hit. You won't be disappointed with the outcome.

Second, you have no promise of anything in this life other than the love of God. Do not forget this and make it the foundation of your marriage. Pray together, worship together, praise together, get to understand our wonderful creator together, grow in God together.

Third, when you say something like, "In sickness and in health" know that that doesn't just mean "when I've been married 40 plus years". That thought did run through my head 2 years ago when Lisa and I got married. I guess the point of this point is that you need to take the promises and vows you make each other seriously. You are going to be standing before a bunch of people, and God, when you say those promises and I would hope that you cherish and remember those vows you make to each other as sacred words before Him. I would hope that would mean far more to you for the rest of your lives than the love you feel for each other now. You love will change, God's love will not.

Finally, know that I love you Adam. I've known you your whole life and while we have taken drastically different paths I wish you and Shelly the best. I would hope that this sickness I am enduring now is simply a venue by which I can get to know you and Shelly much better in the future. Don't be shy, I've got a lot of free time these days, I'm your brother and we can talk about anything.

To close I will leave you in the hands of a far more elegant man than myself, Robert Browning, who summed this whole letter up nicely and finalizes my wish for you both when he said:

"Grow old along with me! The best is yet to be, the last of life, for which the first was made.

Our times are in his hand who saith, 'A whole I planned, youth shows but half; Trust God: See all, nor be afraid!'"

I love you,
Ben

THURSDAY, JULY 12, 2007

Home for a bit!

I HAVE TO ADMIT THAT I'M a little frustrated that it's been a week since I entered the hospital and now I am a bit disappointed that I am scheduled go back to chemo early next week. I'm not really sure what I'm going to do with the next day or two at home, but Lisa and I were planning on the island this weekend. I will very much appreciate a place that is not Virginia Mason.

This morning I had a little break down in front of the Patient Care Technician, Nurse, and Doctor. I really was having issues with no one telling me WHEN I might be leaving and continually prolonging the experience by saying something like, "Oh, you need more blood, or platelets," or,

"Let's wait until tomorrow morning and see what your blood works look like." With the chemo you get an end time. With this one you get to watch and see if they can keep you there any longer than normal.

I probably shouldn't be so cynical, I'm just frustrated with the situation. This is 2 days longer than I've stayed over before. And I'm looking at starting a 5 day chemo session next week. I am tired and need strength.

FRIDAY, JULY 13, 2007

Sometimes rough

LISA AND I ARE HEADING OUT to the island this weekend for a brief little respite again.

It's really strange having lost a week this, errr, past week, what with being in the hospital and all. Home time and hospital time seem like two drastically different things. Now that I'm home it's a little strange to think it's almost been 2 weeks since I last finished chemo vs the 1 it feels like.

I've been kind of emotional as of late, I could use some prayer for strength. I was having a hard time with "normalcy" the other day. It's really hard not being able to plan something very far in advance. I miss working a lot and I'm not sure really what to do with myself some days. I wish I could help out Lisa with some tasks but I don't have the energy for it, or to even be able to bring in some type of income would be good. Anyway, the lack of that has me kind of shaken as of late.

MONDAY, JULY 16, 2007

Don't take my wife

PLEASE. I CAN'T EVEN BEGIN to tell you what she means to me. Lisa has become as important to me these past few months as my own hands. I really wish I could even begin to repay her for her working full time and taking care of me this summer. It's been rough because I can't do the things as a husband that I would be typically doing (working, helping take out the trash, doing other misc. husband support activities) so I know it's been hard on her.

I know two years ago when we stood in front of a lot of you and said our vows to each other that we had no idea we would ever be going through something like this together so soon in our lives together. God however had other plans and has chosen to strengthen the relationship that we have/had already with this event. I don't know what the future holds, but I seriously hope I get the chance to spend many, many more years telling her how much I love and appreciate everything she's done for me.

Lisa I love you so far beyond what I did two years ago. I pray that what God has for the two of us involves many years together, children to pass

His and our love onto, and a platform to tell the world how much God has done for the two of us. My thanks cannot be heartfelt enough or "I love you" said more passionately by me at this time.

Lisa you are the second most important thing in my life, and you have been a rock to me. Thank you.

Chemo round 4?

THIS MORNING BRIGHT AND EARLY I had blood work done to see what all is going on on the inside. Turns out my platelets are too low to administer chemo and they need to be about 3 times higher than they are currently.

I'll be getting blood work done again on Wednesday morning, but the doctor is thinking that it'll be Friday or Monday before I'll be healed enough to start the next round of chemo.

This is both good and bad. I am REALLY going to enjoy the time off I have as right now my strength and energy are at a pretty good level. I can eat and will enjoy being able to do some things this week that I haven't been able to do in a couple of months.

The downside being that this will delay everything another week, but that of course is far better than having them beat me down again with drugs before I'm ready for it.

So I've got a reprieve for a couple of days, we'll see what happens. It would be nice to be able to get in on Thursday, but I guess my bone marrow is a little tired.

MONDAY, JULY 23, 2007

Top 10

HOME INFUSION SERVICES DOESN'T OPEN until 8 am, so I can't call them and make an appointment to have blood drawn until then. So, until that time I have devised a list for you all to enjoy.

The Top 10 things to do, while on Chemo, in the hospital:

1. Hit the "call nurse" button to time their reaction. Repeat numerous times for an average.

2. TV: Try and avoid talk shows, judge shows, and commercials during daytime TV.

3. Listen to MP3 player: Just don't get jumpy when the nurse you called (see 10) a second ago sneaks up on you while you are "rocking out."

4. Nintendo DS Lite: Even though you can play with other people within a good 30 foot radius

who also have a DS there is no one close to my age in the ward and thus makes for a solo gaming experience (something tells me Children's Hospital might be more "fun").

5. Hum little songs to myself.

6. Watch DVDs: Since daytime TV is simply a joke it's time to pull out the DVD player and watch something. Odds are good I'll be asleep in 45 minutes to an hour anyway.

7. Check email from my cell phone: I can read it, but replying is limited to my cell phone numeric keypad. But then again what else is there to do?

8. Reading: Assuming I'm not feeling nauseous I'll feel free to read. Doesn't matter what because I'll most likely be asleep in 10 to 30 minutes from reading.

9. Count the little holes in the stuff on the ceiling.

10. Accept visitors/ phone calls: Easily the best way to burn time in the hospital. Doing any of the above with visitors or just talking is the best way to pass the time. Of course I've had a few instances where someone walks into my room and then says, "Oops, wrong room." So I guess this only applies to visitors I know (or who choose to stay long enough for me to say anything).

SATURDAY, JULY 28, 2007

Oh we're home again... couldn't wait to get home again...

WE'RE BACK. ROUND 4... BING, over. I don't know what it is but transferring from hospital to home often leaves me feeling slightly defeated. Like this whole thing will never end and I'll be doing chemo rounds until who knows when. I'm tired, I feel sick and I really wish there was some sense of "normal" in my life. I know God knows what is best for me so that makes everything that is happening to me seem so confusing. There is so much I want to say and convey but I am tired and slightly frustrated with myself at the moment.

At this point Ben was experiencing regular migraines that involved losing vision and feeling in his arms, followed by intense pain. ER visits weren't usually able to provide much relief. Lisa wrote at the time, "It's so frustrating that no one can help Ben, but we keep crying out to God and believing in His goodness."

AUGUST, SEATTLE

SUNDAY, AUGUST 12, 2007

Aaand we're back!

On Friday I ended up going to work in the morning and working for a few hours, then going to my doctor appointment where I waited 50 minutes to see the doctor beyond my appointment time (oh well, that's what you get when they "squeeze you in at the last moment"). Word is we'll try and see what my blood work looks like in the AM on Monday and see if I am "chemo ready".

I really, honestly, am to a point where I have never wanted to go back to chemo any less than I do now. I feel good, quite good and I feel like I am getting better, stronger again. But then tomorrow, probably, I will go into the hospital where they will hook me up to a machine and start pumping drugs into me. Instead of going out and about during the day I'll be laying in a small room feeling progressively worse. It's just kind of discouraging to only be feeling sick because of the "medicine" they give you.

The ENCOURAGING thing about all of this though is when I sit down and really think about it that God has a plan for me. I don't know what that plan is, or what life after (Lord willing) cancer will look like, but there is a plan. That's about the only thing I've got to hold onto right now.

WEDNESDAY, AUGUST 15, 2007

Little round balls of hope...

No I'm not talking about Dippin' Dots being the cure for cancer, I'm talking about my trip to the Mariners game today. I was reminded today as I sat in left field intently watching the game, as much to avoid stray balls (and thus save my life), as my interest in the game, and I remembered back to my science class in college where we went on a field trip to the zoo.

It was at such a time in my life, shortly after marriage, where Lisa and I had a bit of a "scare" where we thought she might be pregnant for a bit. Anyway, I was cruising around the zoo (it actually started to snow a bit while we were there) looking at various animals when I saw a family (what they were doing there on such a cold day I don't know) pushing/pulling a young child around.

It made me realize that someday I wanted to be able to take a child of mine to the zoo and show them the wonders of the world. I was reminded of this again today as I was dodging stray balls in left field. There were a few younger children at the game and it reminded me, especially with everything I have going on in my life right now, that someday I would like to have children of my own with which to do things like go to a baseball game and avoid stray balls with (like I did today with my Dad, who invited me to the baseball game today).

This comes down to me saying that God has helped me find hope in some of the things I do that might not normally have given me hope. In this case I've wanted to go to a baseball game since getting sick, and today I got to do that (thanks Dad).

Again, I don't know what God has in store for me, but I am hoping that someday God will bless me with a child to share His world with.

MONDAY, AUGUST 20, 2007

Long weekend

THIS NEXT WEEK I WILL (90%) probably be starting chemo. It's hard right now because

I feel really good, I feel like I am healing, and at this point in my life all the "suffering" I've got through has been because of the chemo drugs. It's intimidating to go back to feeling as well as I do and knowing that I will get sick again.

No matter my attitude in the hospital, typically at the end of the chemo, when I am home for the first time in a week or so, my attitude can be pretty bad. I'm horribly tired and my body feels beaten up.

Overall God knows what I need though and whether it is migraines, more time in the hospital, or an extra week off, I can only trust Him and know that He is good and knows what is He is doing in my life far, far better than I do.

What has he won?

BECAUSE YOU'VE GOT THIS RARE disease Ben, you've won an all-expense-paid trip to Virginia Mason! Trip expenses courtesy of Group Health. While at Virginia Mason you'll enjoy 6 days of lying around while little drips of chemicals run into your body. But that's not all! Tell him what else he's won!

That's right, there's more! Hospital food! Technically you can eat as much of this stuff as you like, and hey, room service! Visitors are welcome but this trip is only paid for one. Thanks for playing Ben, and we'll see you at Virginia Mason!

Bing... round 5, start!

THURSDAY, AUGUST 23, 2007

C. H. Spurgeon

-by Lisa-

OUR FRIEND DAN SENT THIS QUOTE of Spurgeon's to Ben, who forwarded it to me for posting. I was really encouraged reading it, as whenever Ben has additional pains I think "God, really? Does he need to suffer more?" This passage answers with a "Yes," full of compassion still.

"This sickness is not unto death."

—John 11:4

"From our Lord's words we learn that there is a limit to sickness. Here is an "unto" within which its ultimate end is restrained, and beyond which it cannot go. Lazarus might pass through death, but death was not to be the ultimatum of his sickness. In all sickness, the Lord saith to the waves of pain, "Hitherto shall ye go, but no further." His fixed purpose is not the destruction, but the instruction of His people. Wisdom hangs up the thermometer at the furnace mouth, and regulates the heat.

The limit is encouragingly comprehensive.

The God of providence has limited the time, manner, intensity, repetition, and effects of all our sicknesses; each throb is decreed, each sleepless hour predestinated, each relapse ordained, each depression of spirit foreknown, and each sanctifying result eternally purposed. Nothing great or small escapes the ordaining hand of Him who numbers the hairs of our head.

This limit is wisely adjusted to our strength, to the end designed, and to the grace apportioned. Affliction comes not at haphazard - the weight of every stroke of the rod is accurately measured. He who made no mistakes in balancing the clouds and meting out the heavens, commits no errors in measuring out the ingredients which compose the medicine of souls. We cannot suffer too much nor be relieved too late.

The limit is tenderly appointed. The knife of the heavenly Surgeon never cuts deeper than is absolutely necessary. "He doth not afflict willingly, nor grieve the children of men." A mother's heart cries, "Spare my child;" but no mother is more compassionate than our gracious God. When we consider how hard-mouthed we are, it is a wonder that we are not driven with a sharper bit. The thought is full of consolation, that He who has fixed the bounds of our habitation, has also fixed the bounds of our tribulation."

FRIDAY, AUGUST 24, 2007

Mesna Blues

I know a room so very small
It's down at the end of a very long hall
It's snugged right between 1579
Which is a number I've never found
sublime

The TV is dark, and so high on the wall
I've a fear of being crushed, should it fall
There is also an image, an image so fine
If it weren't for its size, it would be mine

I'm all done with chemo for this round
But I've got to wait for this mesna,
I might as well choke it down
The mesna drip is so slow

And I want to go home... go home

I am officially done with chemo, however, I have to wait for the kidney/liver protectant (mesna) to complete. The doctor told me this could be sometime tomorrow, "earlier than normal." As it stands, I just want to get out of here. More later.

SEPTEMBER, SEATTLE

SUNDAY, SEPTEMBER 2, 2007

Bravery

THIS MORNING AT CHURCH I HAD a friend of ours tell me that she thought I was brave. Which, of course got me thinking on the nature of bravery. I personally don't feel like I am being brave. But as per dictionary.com I guess I am: "To face something courageously."

I guess I'm not sure how else to face this. I mean do I panic and spend my time freaking out about the fact that I have cancer? Honestly that sounds like a LOT more work and effort that I am putting in right now. I think if I am brave, or courageous, it comes from God. I mean at the start of this I was SCARED, and more than a little bothered by the whole situation, but He has given me an enormous peace about the situation and has helped me through each of my chemos thus far.

If you see any bravery or courage from me know that you are seeing God in my life.

TUESDAY, SEPTEMBER 11, 2007

And the orange stands alone

THE STRANGE PART ABOUT THIS whole cancer/chemo thing has been the not knowing what is going to happen in a couple of days, much less a week or even a month from now. I know none of us REALLY know what will happen in a couple of days or even a month, but it's just more painfully obvious when you are aware of that fact.

I think it's pretty easy to fool ourselves into thinking we know what we are going to do in a couple of days, or weeks, or even 6 months from now. Today is the day that Lisa and I planned 8 months ago to be going to England for 2 weeks. As you all know, we're not going to England. We had to cancel the tickets and our trip plans so that I could try and get better.

We'd like to make plans to go to England again sometime, but at this point in our lives we just don't know what the future holds. So, we'll socket away the money that we were able to scavenge from canceling plane tickets (they charged us 250 per ticket after we canceled!!) and hope that sometime in the future God will bless us with a wonderful trip.

FRIDAY, SEPTEMBER 14, 2007

"You must be Mr. Morrell..."

WHEN I GO INTO A LARGE hospital, much less call a large hospital I don't expect to be expected. This morning I called Virginia Mason and was transferred to "bed control" to see what time I should come in to start chemo.

> Me: "Hello, I'm calling to see what time I should come in today."
>
> Her: "You must be Mr. Morrell."
>
> Me: "Creepy..."
>
> Her: "How about high noon... no scratch that, how about 1."
>
> Me: "Works for me. Thanks."

I can't believe that I am the ONLY person expected to come into Virginia Mason today am I? I don't know... kinda strange when someone from something that big singles you out. That said I've got a few more hours of freedom before the chemo starts up. (Actually probably most of the day... if I don't get in until 1, odds are good I won't be getting chemo until 5 or 7 tonight.)

I view chemo 6 as a kind of last chemical hurdle I have to get over. Chemo 7 we've seen isn't "fun" per se, but it doesn't bring me down as hard as this type of chemo does. So chemo 7 will be a bunch of sitting in the hospital waiting for things to happen. Odds are good I'll even be able to work during the next chemo via remote laptop connection. Thus making this next chemo the "hurdle" to get over because of how it will make me feel for the next couple of weeks.

SATURDAY, SEPTEMBER 15, 2007

The same body

-by Lisa-

"Remember the prisoners, as though in prison with them, {and} those who are ill-treated, since you yourselves also are in the body." Hebrews 13:3

This is the amazing sympathetic kindness that many have shown to us during this time. I am continually nonplussed by the number of people who tell us that they pray for us every day and who demonstrate so much care for us. At first, I just thought that they had serious spiritual discipline in their prayer life, and a serious list of petitions. I thought that maybe for those looking to serve someone, we were a relatively easy target. Still, I was amazed that we made the list with so many people we don't know.

But now, I am beginning to see that for some reason God has laid us on many people's hearts, that for some reason, whether in prayer or not, we come to mind. How can people we don't know feel for us so deeply? Because of God's grace. Until now I have been considering how we can show thanks to everyone who has helped us (because we can't even begin to pay them back). Now, it comes to me strongly that every blessing is directly from God.

Ben and I are not crushed. In fact, we're not anywhere close. Why? Because of the emails, the meals, the prayers, the visitors, the help with rides and housework. All of this is a blessing directly from God, which so many of his servants have been willing and cheerful to carry out. It comes to me that for some reason it is more fruitful in Ben's and my growth to abundantly provide for us than to bring us to a point of desolation and squalor. Many other people have been tried far beyond this, because God saw that it was good. However, God has seen that it is good to make us cared for by his people. I think we'll have a lot to live up to later. After all, God's people are blessed so that they might be a blessing.

WEDNESDAY, SEPTEMBER 19, 2007

Pill color

JUST A SECOND AGO I WAS eating some Key Lime Yogurt when I realized that the color of the yogurt was the same color as the pill I just choked down minutes before. People tell you to eat your greens but I don't think Dexamethasone and key lime yogurt are quite what they had in mind.

On a grand scale of how I am feeling today is not the greatest. I guess pretty much every day after this type of chemo is a kind of downward spiral until I go back into the hospital. But I think perhaps that is not a good way to think about it. God has given me this time at home to do something with and I should be doing that something well, not lamenting the fact that I feel horrible or counting down the number of days until I'm back in the hospital (counting the number of days I am out of the hospital...).

The hardest part about this "time" of chemo is the nights. I'll sleep for a couple of hours (4 or 5) and then be awake for another couple hours, then fall asleep shortly before Lisa gets up for work. I am thinking that possibly I will just get out of bed next time and maybe tire myself out sooner that way than lying in bed. Also the dreams are really bad. Horribly strange dreams that can only be from the drugs. Really not cool or anything I ever want to repeat, but they stay in my head long after I'm awake again.

FRIDAY, SEPTEMBER 21, 2007

My First ABCs of Cancer

A is for Ativan: Which helps with anxiety and in my case nausea.

B is for Bed: Where I spend lots of time (hospital and home).

C is for Chemo: Ranging from short or long.

D is for Dexamethasone: A steroid that takes away the nausea.

E is for Emergency Room: Where they take me when I have pain.

F is for Friends: Who visit while I'm sick.

G is for Groshong: How they give and take fluids from my body.

H is for Hospital: Some are very good and others are not so good.

I is for Internet: Which I should use never to look up any drugs, symptoms, or cancers.

J is for Just this right now: And not time

for anything else (beating cancer).

K is for Killer: That's what cancer can be to you and I.

L is for Leukocytes: Also called white blood cells, they keep me healthy.

M is for Mesna: That protects the kidney and liver from Chemo drugs.

N is for Nurses: Who look after cancer patients like me.

O is for Overly-long stays in the hospital: 7 days is just too much.

P is for Parents: Who support me all the time.

Q is for Questionable: Which describes the Eastside Group Health Hospital.

R is for Radiation: They say I'll have to have this...

S is for Surgery: I'll get it before radiation, to remove the cancer particles.

T is for Tumor: Which resides in my abdomen.

U is for Urgent care: What I get when I don't have an immune system.

V is for Vincristine: A powerful chemo drug.

W is for Wife: Who stays beside me through thick and thin.

X is for X-cancer patient: Is what I want to be!

Y is for You: Who is reading and praying for me!

Z is for Zofram: That takes away the nausea.

Now I know my cancer ABCs next time won't you pray with/for me?

Ben became "neutropenic" (his white blood cells died off) again and checked into the hospital on September 23rd, 2007.

SUNDAY, SEPTEMBER 30, 2007

Long time huh?

LISA AND I ARE OFFICIALLY ON day 8 of my prolonged stay at Virginia Mason. It makes me wonder if they sent me home "early" other times, or if my body is slow to respond this time. Either way I spent 13 days of September in a hospital, which brings my total time in hospital for this summer up to about 60 days. I'm not as impatient as I used to be, something happened between chemo 6 and now. God has really helped me with the patience I need to be a good patient.

OCTOBER, SEATTLE

TUESDAY, OCTOBER 2, 2007

Wherever...

"Wherever you are, be all there. Live to the hilt every situation you believe to be the will of God."

—Jim Elliot

FOUND THIS ON A FRIEND'S Facebook quotes this evening. I believe the cancer in my body has been sent to me by God. I have a semi-hard time with this quote. Can I really "be all there" when I am locked in the hospital for 10 days? Is it possible to keep my mind focused on being IN the hospital when being IN the hospital for that many days is prone to set me into a kind of depression? How does Jim mean "be all there"?

I come home and I am smacked right in the face with the reality that I have just spent 10 days in the hospital. Think back to what you were doing a week ago, I was in the hospital at that point for 3 days. I can't in all honesty reconcile 10 days and the time I spent during those days. Some days I spent sleeping. I don't know how I can make up for days like that. I have no idea how long I am on this Earth, none of us really do, my mortality just seems to have me by the gut, and I have spent at least 60 of the past 150 days in a hospital room. I can only pray God gives me more time healed so I can make up for some (all?) of those 60 days. That is a LOT of alone time, when I could have been with other people. That is a lot of not seeing Lisa when I could have been making her life more wonderful. That is a lot of ME time when I really didn't want it.

I can't justify the time God has given me in the hospital rooms, by myself, and maybe those times aren't for me to justify, but that time still weighs on me.

I have come up with a little something of an acronym to remind me what I have learned from my time in the hospital though: GLO.

Obey God
Cherish Lisa
Love Others

I guess I don't know how else to break it down. I need to remember to do what God says, love Lisa and let her know it, and then love and be kind of people who aren't God or Lisa.

FRIDAY, OCTOBER 5, 2007

Depression and Lies

THE OTHER DAY WHEN I GOT home from the hospital I was depressed. The depression continued to the next day as well. I wasn't thinking about it too hard but I couldn't really put my finger on why I was depressed.

Well, God provides, I got 3 emails which all had clues to my depression in them from separate people and then Lisa came home and told me that being depressed is essentially believing a lie, or lies, about something. So armed with that information I was able to figure out what lies I was believing that were making me depressed.

The first lie was that the past 10 days I had spent in the hospital were wasted and useless. My mom pointed out that I really don't know what God is doing in my life or the lives of others around me. We might never know why I was in the Hospital for 10 days (double the normal time) but God has a purpose and a plan.

The second lie I believed was that I was being an undue burden on Lisa with my sickness. It was pointed out to me by an ex-coworker that marriage isn't always 50/50 and that sometimes the other person (Lisa) is going to have to take care of me. Other times I will have to take care of Lisa. We made vows to this effect when we got married. In sickness or in health we promise to stay by each other's side. I am sick right now, and Lisa hasn't left my side. I thank God for her staying-ness and her wisdom.

The depression lifted with the understanding of the lies I was believing and I have been depression free since then.

THURSDAY, OCTOBER 11, 2007

Better in the Morrell house

I AM OF TWO MINDS ABOUT THIS upcoming scan on Monday. In some ways I want to know how my insides are doing, and in other ways I think I would rather not know. More fear of the unknown. It could be good news, or bad news, either way I find it hard to walk in there because of the potential bad news. The part about this that has really grown my faith in God is the fact that there is really NOTHING I or anyone around me can do to heal me. It is all up to God to heal me. If He has other plans then that is what is going to happen, but this road has been long and strange, and I have more unknown road before me. I pray the Lord heals me and grants me many many more years (I was commenting to my brother the other day that it would be cool to go to his and his wife's 50th wedding anniversary being as I missed their wedding).

MONDAY, OCTOBER 15, 2007

most pain evar

SO THE CT SCAN TODAY WENT well... the time leading UP to the scan however did not go so well. They tried 3 times to get the IV in me (taking about an hour and a half to do it) and it hurt a LOT. Probably the most pain I have experienced since I started all this cancer stuff. They were heat packing my arms and all sorts of stuff. They used a small needle and everything. It was NOT a happy time for me. However I made it through and got the scan and will be waiting until Wednesday for those results.

I got to the hospital about 12 and left at 3. When I got home I just crashed on the couch because my hands hurt from the pokings and needles. The people were excessively nice, though. That is something I appreciate: if the experience is going to be a bad one you might as well remember that the people were nice to you.

WEDNESDAY, OCTOBER 17, 2007

Intimidation

WHILE THE CT SCAN WAS PHYSICALLY painful the trips to see the doctor are mentally/emotionally difficult. So much "bad news" at the start of meeting the doctor really makes me very intimidated to go see him. Even if he has "good news" (healing!!) it takes a lot to walk into that office. The funny thing is that this guy is one of the most mild-mannered people I have ever met, and I'm afraid of seeing/hearing from him.

The last time I had a CT scan was after the 2nd round of chemo, and here we are just shy of the 7th round. After the 2nd there were noticeable results, I am hoping to hear more of that today, but there is still a little voice inside my head that is doom and gloom that says, "Yeah, but what if it's NOT good news." I don't know that I could handle "bad news" right now.

The thing that scares me about this situation I think is that God is, and always has been, completely in control of the situation and I have NO idea what kind of outcome we are looking at. God knows the complete plan and my life is 100% in His hands, but I have to live day to day. I need strength to be able to face the things I fear, and my oncologist is one of those things right now.

It's... news

WELL, AFTER 30 MINUTES OF WAITING and 5 minutes of doctor we have some results. It looks like the tumors haven't shrunk much beyond what they looked like the last time I had a CT scan. The Doctor said however that a CT scan cannot tell them if what they are looking at is cancer or scar tissue (he's guessing more scar than cancer).

Because of the lack of change since the last scan he is in communication now with the surgeon and is making a choice about whether I need a 7th round of chemo or not. So pretty much at this point we continue to wait and see what happens and what the doctors decide.

I at least get another weekend free. The news isn't as great as I had hoped for, but it's not "bad" news per se.

TUESDAY, OCTOBER 30, 2007

fritters

I REALIZED THIS MORNING WHILE I was making fritters that I had chosen the one breakfast item with the most likely possibility to look just like a tumor... on the day that I am going to see the surgeon no less. The sub-conscious is a funny little thing.

Word from the surgeon

THERE WERE SOME COMPLICATIONS with getting the files the surgeon needed to view but a date has been set for my surgery. November 26th is the "big day" and I'll be looking at at least a 6 hour surgery in the "good old fashioned" sense where they open me up and take stuff out.

It was really hard today to talk with the surgeon, he was far from gentle and I came out of it a little freaked out. He hasn't seen any of the scans as of yet so he couldn't say anything to my case specifically but I'll be seeing him again before the surgery.

Things keep piling up with this cancer and it all feels pretty surreal to me. I don't feel sick, is this really happening to me? Lisa reminded me, and in a dazed kind of way I have been hanging onto it, that just because I was reminded how serious my condition was today it doesn't change any of the promises God has given me. This is rough, and really tough at times and in certain places, but I HAVE to cling to God in this. I have nothing else. My mortality is very obviously in God's hands, and as long as He gives me life I will keep fighting for it.

I am typing now because I don't really feel like talking to anyone. I feel fragile, like I might break or something.

WEDNESDAY, OCTOBER 31, 2007

Stat in the box

LIKE A JACK IN THE BOX the statistics about my cancer keep popping up and I don't really think those numbers are really any help to me but that they in fact hinder the healing process (more mentally than physically). I work pretty hard to keep those numbers pushed into a little box in my head so that they don't go swimming around in my head all day long.

Sometimes, like when meeting with doctors, that box breaks open and all that information and data comes spilling out. Then I have to spend the next couple of days remembering that my trust and faith aren't in man's ability to take things out of me and kill bad things in my body. My trust and faith are in God who created my body.

God is in control. With something as bizarrely rare as this cancer is I can't help but wonder at what God is doing in my life. This is a trial by fire and I am curious what the end holds for me.

NOVEMBER, SEATTLE

FRIDAY, NOVEMBER 9, 2007

struggles

AS I GO THROUGH THESE CANCER treatments I am faced with a couple of emotional struggles that make me ask questions. One of these struggles has been with the issue of God being good and kind. It seems from my limited human perspective that if God were good and kind that I would not be suffering from such a rare form of cancer. However I counter myself with all this in knowing that I have a very limited view of life, of just MY life in general.

I guess I can see God's goodness as well in my life when I take a more subtle look at things. Support from people; prayers and food and letters, having medical insurance, catching this when we did. I say this a lot, but it's true: I don't know the outcome of this but I am working hard to be who God wants me to be so that after this I can do what God wants me to do as effectively as He wants me to do it.

TUESDAY, NOVEMBER 13, 2007

Science

I REALLY DON'T HAVE ANYTHING against science, it's God's gift to man to be inquisitive and to discover things about the world around him. To set out to discover the deeper wonders of God's creation. What I DO have a problem with is people who put their sole faith in science. Those people are hard to deal with when it comes to looking at me and my cancer.

I think perhaps not only do I want to survive this thing for my sake and the friends and family around me, but I REALLY want God to prove those people whose faith lies in the numbers wrong. I would love to be able to stand before them completely healed and say something to the effect of, "My God has healed me, and it was in SPITE of your numbers and statistics."

I can't live in those numbers, there is no hope there. However small those numbers are God is in them though. I trust God has a plan for me and while from where I stand I have no idea what that might be, I have more hope in that unknown that in the tangible "numbers" of science.

Lisa and I are off to see the surgeon in less than an hour, he is a man of science. I need prayer that his faith in his numbers won't rattle my hope. My God is bigger than ... well everything, I just need to keep an eye on that and ask that the people I encounter here on Earth do their best at the jobs God has given them (like being a surgeon).

WEDNESDAY, NOVEMBER 14, 2007

Some answers

YESTERDAY'S VISIT WITH THE SURGEON was not as harrowing as I had expected it to be (which in large part is I think because God gave me the strength to hear the things I needed to hear).

The verdict is that the surgeon is assuming he's going to have to remove a little section of my small intestines and possibly remove a bit of my bladder. The scans weren't really good enough for him to be sure on the bladder issue though. Considering the prediction he had made about removing whole organs in our last conversation I think this is a nice improvement. Praise the Lord.

I also discovered how much of the process I will be out and let me tell you it is a good amount of it (there would be NO other way they would get a breathing tube down my throat unless I were solidly unconscious).

We got some idea as well about recovery and it pretty much sounds like I will be in the hospital for about 2 weeks following the surgery in order to allow me to recoup properly. This followed by several weeks at home as well. So, much like school days, it looks like I get December off (not that the thought of having December off to have metal staples hold me together for most of it sounds like FUN mind you. However I wonder if I can get them to use red and green staples, just to be festive and all...).

THURSDAY, NOVEMBER 15, 2007

I'm a tool

IN TODAY'S MODERN LANGUAGE BEING called a "tool" isn't a good thing. It's funny the slang use of the word "tool" means that you are being used (and foolish) and you don't even know it. Is there modern slang for being used AND knowing it?

I know I am being used by God. I don't know to what end that usage will take, but I figure if God wants to use me as a tool that He is probably building His kingdom. I won't get a glimpse of that until after this life, but while I am here I figure I had try and be the best "tool" there is. And you know what, by a bunch of other people's standards I probably will be viewed as a "tool" (modern slang). I guess it's all a matter of perspective. I wouldn't doubt that putting more faith in God than in the doctors probably would seem like foolishness to a lot of people.

Yes, that's right: I'm a tool.

SATURDAY, NOVEMBER 24, 2007

A timid entry

I WAS GREETED THIS MORNING, when I checked my email, by numerous encouragements and well-wishers for my health. It was very encouraging.

God provides. He provides healing, He provides trials to bring us closer to Himself, He provides peace, He provides Doctors, and He provides the support I need in friends and family.

This cancer is the biggest hurdle I have ever had to go through in my life this far. There is no way I can make it over on my own. I know God is there, but I also think He has provided all of you to help me as well.

Am I scared of the surgery ahead of me? Yes I am, the recovery isn't going to be easy, but I ask that you will all pray for healing and strength for me as I go into this.

Ben's surgery was scheduled after Thanksgiving so that he was able to celebrate with his family. The night before the surgery, some family and friends gathered to pray for Ben. He appreciated the intent, though he was still nervous.

TUESDAY, NOVEMBER 27, 2007

The Surgery Report!

-by Lisa-

THE SURGERY WENT AMAZINGLY, awesomely, wonderfully well!

Well, the scenario wasn't the cool miraculous possibility that Ben and I half-joked about, that the surgeon (Dr. Mann) would open him up and *Voila* no tumors left! But, there are no tumors now!!

So we checked in at 10:45am as scheduled. The surgery didn't really start until 1pm, or possibly 1:30 depending on how you define "start," but they kept Ben pretty busy with a little paperwork, questions about allergies, the epidural insertion, etc. He was definitely shaking as he anticipated what was about to happen, but as my dad pointed out later in the day, even Jesus got nervous anticipating trials to come :)

Ben's parents, my parents, me, and Beth (for awhile, until she went back to school) waited in the "surgery waiting room," which has THE phone. Every couple hours a nurse would call and give us an update, which put us more at our ease as we waited in the comfy armchairs, talking and occupying ourselves in various other ways.

Less than 6 hours later, Dr. Mann walked in and gave us his report! There were hundreds of tiny tumors in Ben's abdomen, but he had removed them all-- praise God! That was one of my worries, but it was solved. AND, amazingly, none of the intestine or bladder had to be removed, so the digestive tract is completely *intact*! That meant that Ben didn't need to go to the ICU at all, but was able to be transferred straight from Recovery to the hospital. Also, his recovery will be quicker, and there will be less concerns about him eating!

I laughed when I heard what Dr. Mann did remove: Ben's appendix! Of all the organs in his abdomen that could be completely ridden with tumors, that was it, which is so cool! Many people have them easily removed and live in normal health without them. No appendicitis for Ben. Also, Dr. Mann removed a little of Ben's liver, which isn't a big deal.

He told us that the large tumor between Ben's bladder and rectum was about the size of a baseball, or maybe a little larger, and difficult to remove. Fortunately he was able to take it out and only scraped the walls of bladder and rectum, which required a little "patching" but not "resectioning."

After we heard the results we waited around a bit more, then found Ben's hospital room and waited there until he arrived from Recovery. When he got wheeled into the room, I was surprised to see that his eyes were open and that he was talking! Coherently! He was feeling a little nauseous and had additional tubing protruding from his body, but he seemed to be feeling pretty well otherwise. We happily told him about how well the surgery had gone. He said that he had some interesting dreams during the surgery and was irritated to be woken up from them by a pain in his stomach.

So, to wrap this up, praise God! I'm so glad he responded to our prayers with affirmatives and that we can praise him for that!

DECEMBER, SEATTLE

FRIDAY, DECEMBER 7, 2007

this (fragile) tent

I'VE COME TO REALIZE THESE past few months that the flesh that we cling to so firmly to is really a very fragile tent. It's not hard at all to damage it or to somehow put a serious hole in it. Then when you damage it, it takes so long to repair.

It's scary to be how fragile I am, and I wish I wasn't so frail. It really serves as a reminder that I am more than just this set of flesh and blood. That I have an immortal inside that can live forever. God has given us souls that are to endure much longer than the flesh tent they are currently housed in.

This reminder to me serves two purposes: 1. All life is precious, and everyone has a soul. 2. No matter what might happen to my "tent" right now, I know that the insides are guarded and watched over my God so no matter how tattered the tent might become the insides are what count.

Ben had about a month and a half to recover from surgery before he started radiation treatments.

THURSDAY, DECEMBER 20, 2007

The Goods

YESTERDAY AFTER DROPPING LISA off at work I made the trek down to the Seattle waterfront to the Edgewater hotel. There I got to participate in the Taproot Theatre Company Christmas party. It seems for the past few years they have all gotten excited about the eggs benedict that the Edgewater makes up so they bring in trays of the stuff. I however am not a fan of eggs or benedict, so I simply contented myself with the breakfasty potatoes and various assorted pastries (my appetite still not being what I wish it was I don't think I really made any kind of dent in either the pastries OR the potatoes).

Following the breakfast was the annual white elephant gift exchange. It's a chance to get rid of things that would be classified just above trash (or possibly "pretty trash" or "working trash") and to see how we juggle it around the room and laugh at some of the outrageous things that people paid money for at one time in their lives and also to see what kinds of trash gifts people will fight over. All this would be an interesting social study in any environment, but add to the fact that these people are drama/ theatre people and the entertainment level goes up a few notches.

Following my trip to Seattle I booked it back to this side of the lake and had lunch with Adam, my friend at Google (you know, the one who has been pressuring me to submit an application/ resume to Google? {With friends like these who needs a temp agency!}). Now I have only been in 1 Google building but the contrast from the (numerous) Microsoft buildings I have been in was... dare I say extreme? The general types of people in such places seemed about the same but the environment was way different from MS (I don't know how much I am allowed to talk about so I will keep it short).

Anyway, I think I discovered yesterday if I plan on working for a large mega-corp it'll need to be more like MS and less like Google in the environment. I really would have a very hard time working in that type of environment (plus I think I am starting to learn that I have a serious like for Non-profits, so I think I'll keep my hat here in the non-profit ring for now).

Last night Lisa got a call from John, an older friend, about a project that might be happening (or not) and I got to talk to him for a while as well. He's the only person I have talked to so far that has been through radiation treatments. He gave me some tips and suggestions. I think it'll probably be a little rougher than I expect right now, but at only 2 weeks of it I don't think I'll have a problem making it through.

MONDAY, DECEMBER 24, 2007

Pre-Christmas Cheer

LISA AND I SPENT A WONDERFUL weekend up on the island with Lisa's folks and sisters. We are spending Christmas with my family so Christmas Eve (today) is going to be spent with my in laws.

Healing wise things are going really well, strange as it sounds my abdomen area just feels like it has been sunburned (and thus cloth rubbing against it is a bit grating but I assume that will continue to heal as time goes on as well).

It's strange to be starting to gear up for a whole new year. Earlier this year I wasn't entirely sure I would be seeing a new year and everything that brings. Praise the Lord we have made it this far and Lisa and I are starting to plan a few things for the start of the new year.

2008

JANUARY, SEATTLE

TUESDAY, JANUARY 1, 2008

God's Faithfulness is a Scar

"Love's as hard as nails,
Love is nails:
Blunt, thick, hammered through
The medial nerves of One
Who, having made us, knew
The thing He had done,
Seeing (with all that is)
Our cross, and His."

— C.S. Lewis

GREATLY, DEEPLY

GOD'S FAITHFULNESS IS EVIDENT IN the world around us if we take the time to stop and look for it. The atheist might argue that there is no God simply because they cannot see evidence of Him. I would disagree and say that if you take the time to stop and look around all the "coincidences" of life are more than just the sum of chance.

God's faithfulness to man isn't always "pretty," clean, or safe. Take Jesus for example: What was his goal in coming to Earth? To die as a sacrifice for the sins of mankind. This is the faithfulness of God that had been prophesied to the Jews for hundreds of years. Jesus bears the scars from the Father's faithfulness. His hands and side all bear the scars that are a sign of the Faithfulness that God provided mankind.

I was reminded, and will forever be reminded, of God's faithfulness to me and Lisa because of the scar that I bear as well. Around 10 inches of scar where the surgeon took out the tumors in my body.

It wasn't a painless procedure, and I will most likely bear the scar for the rest of my life, but it serves as a reminder to this past year and everything God has done to be faithful to Lisa and I. He is working in us and He will not suddenly give up the work He has started.

SUNDAY, JANUARY 13, 2008

Such and Such

"Come now, you who say, 'Today or tomorrow we will go to such and such a city, and spend a year there and engage in business and make a profit.' Yet you do not know what your life will be like tomorrow. You are just a vapor that appears for a little while and then vanishes away. Instead, you ought to say, 'If the Lord wills, we will live and also do this or that.'"

—James 4:13-15, NASB

FRIDAY NIGHT, AND SATURDAY as I was lying in bed in the dark, the above verse came to mind. I have to confess that getting migraines or some other such medical malady when I have plans is really frustrating.

However this past year I have learned a lot about planning and what will actually happen. I get frustrated because it seems "unfair" that I have a migraine when I have so many other things going on in my life at the same time. I even pull out the excuse, "How could this happen? It's my birthday!" As if that makes any kind of difference. "If the Lord wills" has been a rallying cry this past year but, like many people I am prone to forgetfulness. Maybe I should get it tattooed on my arm (HA! Needles... right).

It turned out that Ben's string of migraines (which sent him to the ER three times in three days) were likely due to an infection inside his Groshong – the small tube going into his chest for IV infusions and blood draws. The best course of action was to remove it. To Ben's surprise, instead of using a formal surgical procedure the nurse yanked it out of his chest without any warning!

SATURDAY, JANUARY 26, 2008

like pulling...

TEETH HAVE GOT **NOTHING** ON a well put in Groshong (note I have had BOTH pulled in my life, so I speak from experience). It would be a toss-up as to whether I wanted teeth pulled or a Groshong pulled out again. I guess the Groshong DID go faster, but it feels like someone is sticking their finger through my chest right now.

But, by the grace of God in a few days I will be able to take a complete shower again! No more having to worry about getting the little lines wet, and God graced me with the strength to make it through the day. It's been a long week, but it is over and Lord willing we can get back to the healing process.

Ben Morrell

SUNDAY, JANUARY 27, 2008

Sometimes I think of heaven

DURING CHEMO AND RECOVERY from surgery I didn't much think about "my end destination" as it were. I spent a lot of time focusing on doing what I needed to do to get better and heal up.

More recently I have been thinking about the world after this world. Thinking a bit about what God has promised: no more tears, or pain. I don't know that that had much appeal to me before this last year. Knowing there would be no more pain is one thing when you haven't had a lot of pain in your life, but after going through such intense chemo and then such a serious surgery, it got me to thinking more about what I am going through here on Earth.

MARCH, SEATTLE

The recovery from radiation was rougher and took longer than Ben and Lisa expected. Because the cancer treatments were finished, they thought that "normal" life would resume almost immediately. In fact, they had planned to be part of a mission trip to Guatemala at the end of the week Ben finished his treatment! The day before the trip, Ben's doctor said that would be too dangerous, so they canceled it at the last minute. This turned out to be fortunate, because for the better part of the next two weeks Ben and Lisa were both pretty sick.

MONDAY, MARCH 3, 2008

A Break from Bellevue

DOCTOR'S VISIT THIS WEEK. Time for the radiologist to take a look at me and say, "Wow... you need to gain some weight!" Yes, thank you, I am working on that.

I have a confession as well, recently in my "down times" or if my mind starts to wander I find myself dreading my upcoming appointment in April with the oncologist. Is the cancer gone? Will I be forced to start this horrible process all over again? Sometimes I feel like I just don't want to know. But reminding myself that God is in control is pretty much what gets me through those times. It's scary not being in control and having something so very close to remind you of that.

THURSDAY, MARCH 6, 2008

Radiation is a warm puppy...

I WAS INFORMED YESTERDAY AT the meeting with the Radiologist that the kind of radiation I was put through was, "One of the roughest we do here." Oh... great (this might also explain the glowing at night and/ or the low platelet count).

Anyway, they poked me and prodded me yesterday and looked me over and said, "You are looking good!" Patted me on the head, told me to gain weight and sent me home (with blessing to go on a road trip in the middle of the month).

In mid-March, Ben and Lisa took a road trip along the west coast to see family and friends. About halfway through the trip, in Los Angeles, Ben got shingles.

Shingles is a viral rash. It was painful enough that Ben flew to Seattle and stayed with his parents while Lisa drove back with her father.

MONDAY, MARCH 24, 2008

Another day in bed

YESTERDAY WHEN MY GRANDMOTHER was over she took to calling me "Job" I appreciate the sentiment, but there is a LOT of stuff Job went through that I REALLY do not want to go through. For this fact I am glad God promises to never give us more than we can bear... makes me kind of impressed He's trusted me with so much thus far. I wonder what He wants me to do with it?

TUESDAY, MARCH 25, 2008

Home a little early

THIS CANCER, AND RELATED ISSUES, has really taught me a lot about a subject I already thought I knew a lot about: flexibility. People are amazingly flexy, the alternative, really, is snapping like a dried twig. You never really get to see how much you can "bend" until God sends stuff your way that you don't think you could ever handle.

Also the more we stretch and flex the more we CAN stretch and flex, so what seemed like something really tough and difficult before becomes something we have already been through or gone past. Of course I doubt that going through another round of chemo, surgery, and radiation would be easy now, but the idea of having cancer is a little more... settled(?) than it was a year ago.

I want to encourage you, no matter what you feel like you're being "bent" through right now to stay strong and no matter what remember that God loves you, and He is the only one that can see the full plan that is best for us and those around us.

APRIL, SEATTLE

FRIDAY, APRIL 4, 2008

Reminders

"Yet in all these things we are more than conquerors through Him who loved us. For I am persuaded that neither death nor life, nor angels nor principalities nor powers, nor things present nor things to come, nor height nor depth, nor any other created thing, shall be able to separate us from the love of God which is in Christ Jesus our Lord."

— Romans 8:37-39 (NKJV)

I have been reminded these past couple of days from a few "random" sources that God loves me and has my refinement in mind for me through all that I have been going through. I read through Romans 8 tonight and was reminded of so many of God's promises to us in trials and tribulation. I would encourage you to read it over, it is a worthwhile thing to do.

I think these messages are coming at an appropriate time as my meeting with the oncologist gets closer and I have to really honestly face what is going on inside my body. I think God is trying to remind me of the things I read tonight in Romans 8. No matter what the outcome nothing (cancer) can separate me from God's love. It has been hard, it will be hard, but God has something for me. I hope I'm paying enough attention to Him to know what it is.

A CT scan in April was the first check for cancer after the completion of Ben's treatments. Ben was always anxious about meeting with the doctor, and even more so on this occasion.

WEDNESDAY, APRIL 16, 2008

It's back... (Good News!!)

TO A CANCER FREE LIFE!? Our appointment today was amazing. We checked in at 4pm, and we were into and had seen the doctor and were out again at 4:30. Pretty impressive.

The other thing that was pretty impressive was the scan. The doctor couldn't see anything out of the ordinary. Everything looked just fine to him. The word "remission" was tossed about as well (I even LOOKED at the scans myself this time... pretty cool).

My blood counts are still low, but the doctor said it can take 6 months to a year for those to come back to normal after what I have been through and he's not worried about that.

I guess I am still in a bit of shock. I pretty much was trying NOT to expect the worst, but I was. I got the complete opposite of the worst news, I got the best news.

My prayer before I went in was that if the news was good I wouldn't slip into mediocrity in my life, and if the news was bad that I wouldn't let it affect my attitude. Well, the news was good, so it looks like I have a more difficult task ahead of me.

FRIDAY, APRIL 18, 2008

The other side

I HAVE TO ADMIT IT'S BEEN KIND of strange these past few days knowing for the moment that I am cancer free. It's been just about a year now since I was told the opposite news (and all but handed a brochure on coffins) and I've been laboring away this past year to remedy the situation. Now here I am with the news that I (we) had been praying for.

Of course I still am just as weak as I was before the news, hearing the information didn't suddenly give me the strength I had lost, so it's kind of sinking in slowly. I am very thankful for everyone's excitement around me though. I can't think of better news honestly.

This last year I prayed very strongly for healing, and I continue to pray for it, so being as God has answered some of my prayer I think it only appropriate to spend this year fervently thanking Him as well (of course we should ALWAYS thank God for everything, but while 25 was the year of Cancer, and praying for healing, 26 is going to be themed the year of Thanks).

WEDNESDAY, APRIL 23, 2008

Traveling...

"When going through hell, keep on going."

— Winston Churchill

I FOUND THE ABOVE WINSTON Churchill quote half a year ago or so and I thought it really spoke to my situation. Even though I was, am, and could be, going through a tough time (the more earthly version of "hell," much less the real thing) God has given me the strength for right now to keep on going. That is a major "take away" (a nod there to you corporate lingo types {MS'er I'm looking at you}) from this illness has been to work on today.

God will give me the strength to face next week... when I get to next week. Right now He's giving me the strength I need for now. He's outside of time, but I am not.

I also found this quote inspirational because sometimes when I have been faced with some of this cancer treatment I honestly don't want to go on sometimes. This past week when I was thinking about possibly having to go through chemo again I was kicking around the idea a time or two of seriously rejecting the "treatment." I don't have to make that choice this time around, and God knows what is best for me. So at this point I will continue to strive on this Earth until He gives me further notice.

MAY, SEATTLE

SUNDAY, MAY 18, 2008

Onward!

TODAY FINDS LISA AND I searching out more of what we are going to be doing with our lives as I continue to get stronger and, Lord willing, getting on with the lives we have been given.

Until just recently I was thinking about putting a lot of my life effectively "on hold" until I found out more about what was going on inside my body, but then I realized I could spend the rest of my life doing that. Always waiting until the NEXT doctor's appointment to do something and hoping that the cancer doesn't come back.

Well, I've decided right now that until the cancer DOES come back I am going to act like it is well and truly gone. Until I hear otherwise I am a survivor and I am going to get on with my life and the things God has for me to do! Onwards I say! I mean honestly, if I spent my time worrying about things that would kill me it would be a full-time job. God has a plan for me and I don't want to hinder that plan because of fears in my life.

JUNE, SEATTLE

SUNDAY, JUNE 1, 2008

Unknowns

It's kind of funny (not of the "haha" variety) that I try not to think too much about the future because if this past year has taught me anything it's that I have pretty much no idea what is going to come my way. I can't help but wonder however, at what point am I more "free" to move around? I mean I've kicked around the idea of getting another job (something full-time so as to not have to do the whole "3 jobs at once" thing) but what happens if I start up another job in the next 3 to 6 months and the cancer makes a come-back? I doubt that the job I'll be in will be anywhere as forgiving as the ones I have now. But then again I don't know that for sure.

I kind of feel like I should be actively moving on with my life, but I am held back by some fears about my health. Valid concerns? Or not?

As usual it's something that God will provide for. If I'm to go on to a bigger/different job it's got to be God's timing anyway. I guess if you really sit down and think about it a normal "healthy" person has just as many unknowns as someone like me who has faced cancer. I'll have to think on the whole thing more.

TUESDAY, JUNE 24, 2008

Who needs a car...

I BEEN HAVING A LOT OF DREAMS LATELY. Last night specifically I had a dream that I had to go into surgery again. It was strange because it happened in my dream just like it did in real life. In my dream I kind of "blacked out" at a certain point and only remember after I woke up. At this point in my life I am trying really hard not to think about what I went through last year. I don't think I would say that I am "out of the woods" by any stretch of the imagination, but it is kind of nice to have the time that God has given me to see people and do things to help people.

I don't know if this has anything to do with being shut in a hospital for so much of last summer, but I have also had quite the desire to travel these last few months. I want to go out and see the world. I'm sure that probably has something to do with being faced with the possibility that I might NOT get to travel when I am "older."

It seems to me like traveling is a two sided coin. On one hand you get to experience new places and new people and expand you horizons, on the other hand it keeps you from close friends and family. The dichotomy of travel.

AUGUST, SEATTLE

WEDNESDAY, AUGUST 6, 2008

Not always as planned...

LISA AND I SPENT TIME WITH the high school group this weekend. Lisa asked me to meet with one of the girls, whose mother has cancer.

It was interesting talking to her for a bit, and I really feel like God can use me through conversations like that, even if it's just to be a completely sympathetic listening ear, but it was probably the hardest thing I have done this week. Talking, remembering, and chatting about Cancer isn't something I feel like I am overly prepared for at this point.

TUESDAY, AUGUST 26, 2008

Letting the bird out of the cage

I AM IN THE PROCESS OF WORKING with a missions organization (OCi) to possibly fill their soon-to-be vacant "Director of Internet Services" position. Lisa and I are still praying and thinking it over, but the job would require a move. A move to Colorado Springs, Colorado.

For those of you wondering about my medical condition, I feel like my oncologist had some really good advice that applies in this case: "Don't let your medical situation stop you from doing what you feel like you need to do." In my case it might be modified to: "Don't let your medical condition stop you from doing what God wants you to do."

As for time frame we'd probably be looking at sometime in October. They have said they'd like me October 1st, but I don't know if that is possible with everything that comes from moving to a new state.

OCTOBER, NOVEMBER, and DECEMBER, COLORADO SPRINGS

Ben did accept the IT Director position in Colorado Springs—his dream job! He and Lisa moved to Colorado in mid-October, 2008.

THURSDAY, OCTOBER 30, 2008

Never Forget

TODAY THE IT DEPARTMENT AND the finance department took an extended lunch to meet and hang out a bit with the new VP of "Global Missions" here at OC. They just spent the last 20 or so years in Africa and have returned. They served us some traditionally Africa dishes for lunch. How was it? Well, I'm full. I didn't have to stop by Wendy's on the way back from work or anything.

While we were there the VP's wife quoted something, and I think she was quoting it about leaving friends behind in Africa, but she said, "We will never forget, but someday it won't hurt to remember."

I was pretty impressed by that quote. It's how I want to feel about cancer. Someday, I don't want it to hurt to remember it.

MONDAY, NOVEMBER 10, 2008

PR

I FEEL LIKE I HAVE BEEN HIT in a really huge way the past day and a half on cancer issues (mentally, not physically). It's really brought my stress level up to some distracting levels. It seems like everywhere I turn I am reminded of cancer (not to mention just looking down at my abdomen).

TUESDAY, DECEMBER 16, 2008

Not always as planned...

SOMETHING THAT I THINK I am prone to forgetting that I was reminded of this evening: Things often don't go as planned.

Aubrey, a friend of mine, an old co-worker,

someone who had had cancer before me, has to go in for chemo and radiation starting on Christmas Eve. Last time she just had surgery and went without the chemo and the radiation... so this will be new for her. We're about the same age.

It's times like these that I yearn for Heaven... because despite the fact that I came through the last trial I did, it was only by the grace of God. I honestly don't know what I would do if I was faced with that option again... knowing what it's like.

2009

JANUARY, FEBRUARY, and MARCH, COLORADO SPRINGS

SATURDAY, JANUARY 10, 2009

27

I GUESS MY HOPE FOR A LOT of my birthdays is that the year following them doesn't end up as... I don't want to say "difficult" because that's not what I really mean, difficultly grows a person, and ease of life doesn't grow your character.

I guess what I really want is for life to come at me, and that I am adequately prepared to handle it, to grow from it, and to be alive on the other side to encourage other people to keep up. (However, even that statement isn't quite right sometimes, because honestly living itself can be a real pain sometimes. {4 migraines in 1 week comes to mind}).

Here is what I would like from my 27th year: I would like to be able to make wise choices when it comes to how I live and know that God has me here, and alive, right now for a reason. And to know that if 27 happens to be the time that God would choose to call me home that it is by His grace and mercy that that would happen and that I would, until that point, live strongly, with purpose, keeping my eyes on my final goal (Heaven) but not lose sight of the people around me and how I can help them as well.

MONDAY, FEBRUARY 9, 2009

Pain and Where God wants me

THIS WEEKEND I GOT A MIGRAINE. It started on Saturday afternoon while Lisa and I were looking at furniture (not a cop-out, I swear) and proceeded to last beyond the normal 24 hours and into this (Monday) morning. It was a painful weekend, and a weekend that I was supposed to help (on Sunday) lead a table discussion at church. This was to be Lisa and I's entrance into service at our new church. I instead stayed home and tried to ignore the virtual baseball bat hits to my brain.

This got me to thinking, and I've wondered this before: If I am doing something that I am pretty sure God wants me to be doing and I am crippled by something like my health where I can't do that thing, what is the point of that? I know God can do anything (including keeping things like migraines and cancer away) but why throw a health curve ball (wow, two sports allusions in one blog post, I must be out of it) at me when I'm about to do something like serve at church, or plan new technology for OC?

I honestly don't know what to do with this. I mean I feel like God has called us here to Colorado Springs, and I genuinely love my job, so things like illness frustrate me. I mean it's not like I can really "slow down" when I have a migraine and reexamine my life. I have to spend as much time as possible asleep so I don't go crazy with head-pain (and/or throwing up).

I guess I'm not looking for THE ANSWER to why I have medical issues, it's just that things like this weekend confuse me. Is there something I need to learn from all this? I know I am not the first missionary to go out onto the field and get sick, so what lessons were learned through the pain of waiting out illness?

Is it something to do with pride? (Doesn't everything come back to that eventually?) DO I need to adjust something? Or is this just "my thing"? "Oh yeah, I get migraines..."

I guess I ask all this because I feel like my mind and spirit want to go about 300mph and all my body can do is a poky 25mph in the school zones. I feel like I could get a lot more done if it wasn't for sicknesses that arise.

MONDAY, FEBRUARY 23, 2009

Follow up 2009 Part A

I WAS PLEASANTLY SURPRISED ONCE Lisa and I finally met the doctor (maybe 30 minutes late?) this morning. He was young, funny, personable, and had seen this type of cancer before. AND he didn't doom and gloom me ("Wow... you should be dead now!" or "Geeze, we'll need scans every 3 months to keep an eye on that sucker!").

He thought that considering the amount of "stuff" I had been through that I was looking really good. I guess the kind of recovery from that regime can take a while and have some very permanent side effects. All I can say to that is praise GOD for the blessings of my health. When it's just me I never really know how I am doing because of the way I am feeling, etc. The doctor helps a bit with a comparison of other people (which I typically don't like) but gave me hope in this instance.

I'm going to have a CT scan sometime this week (wow, you mean I don't have to book 3-6 weeks in advance!?) and then I'll get those results, but the doc thinks I am looking pretty good, so he's positive.

He's also had some experience with this kind of cancer before and knows some other people that have as well, and says he would have done the exact same "stuff" to me as Group Health did so that is good to know as well.

MONDAY, MARCH 2, 2009

Worthy

CT SCAN THIS MORNING.

It didn't really bother me this weekend, I lived life normally, and received a LOT of encouragement from various sources. Today I have been fairly calm, but the having to drink the oral contrast 2 hours ahead of time is a REALLY early reminder of what I am doing. I don't think it's the process (the contrast {oral and injected}, the IV, the scan, etc.). It's the waiting for results.

A very, very great part of me wants to be able to rejoice and celebrate about news that the scan is clear, and I have already dared to imagine what that might look like. If the scan doesn't come back clear though am I in any less of a position to rejoice and celebrate our God? He's in control either way, and I have made daily petitions to Him to heal me, and I am going to get some of that answer sometime this week.

I feel like I am at a fork in my future. I could continue to do what I have been doing with OC and learning to live here in Colorado Springs, or I could go back to all sorts of crazy medical stuff.

It's a rough line I am wandering right now

mentally. If the tumors show up again it's pretty much par for the course for this sickness, and I guess I won't be overly surprised. But I have this hope in the Lord that He can do great things, and that He is the great healer and I have this feeling that He isn't done with me just yet.

But, as I said before, does any of that really get thrown out of the window if the scan doesn't come back clear? I am heavily trying to avoid the "I'll praise you and worship you Lord if the scan is clear." I think that is some of the battle that rages in me: Knowing that God is good and worthy to be praised. No matter what.

MONDAY, MARCH 9, 2009

Free!

THIS MORNING HAS BEEN FULL OF tears for me. Tears of relief and joy and thanksgiving.

I got an email this morning from my doctor saying that the CT scan was free of things that shouldn't be in my abdomen. Praise the LORD!

MAY through AUGUST, COLORADO SPRINGS

SATURDAY, MAY 23, 2009

Way beyond Normal

IT'S EARLY... VERY EARLY. 3AM always seems to hit when you least expect it to. Sleep is like a freeway of time, I get on when I go to bed, and then I take the exit ramp in the morning and resume time in the normal way. Sometimes though I end up taking a wrong turn and wander around the suburbs of "normal time" by being awake at 3am. The rest of the world freeways through time in their sleep and here I am trying to find my way back.

As I was trying to find my way back to sleep

I was catching up on some of the internet I have missed due to working. Jon Acuff over at the blog Stuff Christians Like posted a brief little snippet from his father's blog about faith.

His father said, "I don't want a life that requires much faith."

The general gist of the idea is that the natural state of people is to want security, and when you are secure in something it doesn't require you to have faith in God.

I've been kind of thinking around this idea myself ever since I've had cancer. I sometimes wonder if life would be so much easier without God. If I could simply live in one place, raise a family quietly, you know the "American Dream" thing. But then I get to thinking about it, do I really want to live like everyone else? Do I want to "live quietly"? Do I want to accept "normal"?

At the tough times yes. I do look yearnfully at the supposed "peace" that other people have in normalcy. But you know what? That is one of the great things about faith. God is going to use me, put me in places I don't want to be. Grow me, stretch me, push me to do things I would never "normally" do. And He's going to give me His peace while I am there.

It's going to seem like craziness to the world when you are doing something that requires you leave "normal" behind and do what God has asked you to do, but that is where faith comes in. While I might at times want a life that doesn't require faith, I also don't want a life without God. God will take you and I much further in life than we ever even dreamed was possible, and that takes faith. And that creates an amazing story that God will use.

"...so that Christ may dwell in your hearts through faith—that you, being rooted and grounded in love, may have strength to comprehend with all the saints what is the breadth and length and height and depth, and to know the love of Christ that surpasses knowledge, that you may be filled with all the fullness of God.

Now to him who is able to do far more abundantly than all that we ask or think, according to the power at work within us, to him be glory in the church and in Christ Jesus throughout all generations, forever and ever. Amen."

-Ephesians 3:17-21 (ESV)

In Colorado, Ben and Lisa made new friends, bought a townhouse, went camping, and found a church. Lisa got a job, and the future seemed bright in their new home.

MONDAY, AUGUST 31, 2009

Scanning

WELL, I GUESS IT HAD TO COME eventually. Wednesday, 10:00am is my... well I lost count, but I have another CT scan. It's funny how many of these I have had and for the life of me the one that sticks in my head the most is the first one I ever had. It was a pretty horrible experience. But I had never had an IV put in before and I think the guy who was doing it was probably attempting to do it with his eyes shut. It was just a bad time all around I think.

But here we are on the other side of that and I expect the last experience I had, although it was the most costly CT scan I have ever had, will help this one not seem so bad.

It still creates that kind of rift though until you find out the results of the scan. Either I am going to be dealing with cancer, or I will be "fine" and continue doing what I am doing. The difference between them is huge.

I think some people mistake what I am feeling as fear. I'm not afraid of either outcome, granted chemo was bad, and I never want to go through it again, but I don't think I'm at the point where I would fall apart if I had it again. It wouldn't be pleasant... but it would require me to do a lot more thinking, and obviously it would be what God had chosen for me to go through right now. So being as God knows what is best for me I am awaiting the results hopefully before the end of the week.

SEPTEMBER, COLORADO SPRINGS

WEDNESDAY, SEPTEMBER 2, 2009

Biopsy tomorrow

-by Lisa-

BEN HAD HIS SCAN TODAY and, while his abdomen is clear, there are abnormally inflamed lymph nodes in his lungs.

The doctors are not sure what this means, but it does concern them with Ben's medical history so they will be doing a biopsy tomorrow. We're unsure of the time at the moment.

We're both freaked out and in shock right now...

FRIDAY, SEPTEMBER 4, 2009

The Hardest week Ever

BEING TOLD YOU HAVE CANCER, what kind of cancer, and your odds of survival all in one fell swoop is something I don't think I will ever forget. The excitement and joy at discovering, every time, that you are free of the hell that is cancer treatment is also something I will never forget. Both are things I can pull up at any time and are fresh in my mind.

So the broncoscopy I had today did not tell me what I wanted to hear. Did not tell me anything remotely relating to what I wanted to hear. The quick little in and out procedure was supposed to say, "Oh, you have Bronchitis, nothing more." Instead they said, "While we can't be completely certain until we get this back from pathology the stuff we pulled out of you looks cancerous."

I'll know for certain on Wednesday when I meet with my oncologist what the deal is and what we're looking at doing, but until then I'm on my own with just that information.

I honestly don't even know what to think. Do I want to go through Chemo again? No, not now, not ever again. Do I want to be clear and this not be anything serious? You bet.

How do I react to God in this? I feel like I got a very clear leading to come to Colorado Springs and work with OC and attempt to further the technology. Granted nothing was ever promised to me about my health but I felt like God would protect me through the health issues so I could advance OC with technology that could help further HIS kingdom in the world. Why this? Why now? We're at such a crucial time and this happens.

I know God's in control, but I need something here, I've never felt so hopeless, so much like throwing in the towel and saying, "Fine, I'll do what I feel like I've been called to do until I drop dead."

Dear Lord, I need something to get me through this, something to cling to, or to even know if it's worth clinging.

TUESDAY, SEPTEMBER 8, 2009

Waiting, Day 5

I WOKE UP THIS MORNING ALREADY worried about tomorrow. Being as I hadn't actually been awake yet and I woke up worried I assumed it was the dreams I can't remember that fueled this morning's panic session.

Then I headed over to BibleGateway.com and their verse of the day was from Psalm 143 and I was curious about the context so I pulled up the whole chapter and read it. I think Psalm 143 is the verse for me in this waiting period. I would pull out certain verses to highlight, but as I look at it I just want to paste the whole thing here.

1. Lord, hear my prayer, listen to my cry for mercy; in your faithfulness and righteousness come to my relief.
2. Do not bring your servant into judgment, for no one living is righteous before you.
3. The enemy pursues me, he crushes me to the ground; he makes me dwell in the darkness like those long dead.
4. So my spirit grows faint within me; my heart within me is dismayed.
5. I remember the days of long ago; I meditate on all your works and consider what your hands have done.
6. I spread out my hands to you; I thirst for you like a parched land.
7. Answer me quickly, Lord; my spirit fails. Do not hide your face from me or I will be like those who go down to the pit.
8. Let the morning bring me word of your unfailing love, for I have put my trust in you. Show me the way I should go, for to you I entrust my life.
9. Rescue me from my enemies, Lord, for I hide myself in you.
10. Teach me to do your will, for you are my God; may your good Spirit lead me on level ground.
11. For your name's sake, Lord, preserve my life; in your righteousness, bring me out of trouble.
12. In your unfailing love, silence my enemies; destroy all my foes, for I am your servant.

WEDNESDAY, SEPTEMBER 9

The end of waiting

WELL, THE WAITING ENDED today, 9/9/09 at 9am. My old cancer is back. My abdomen is free of the cancer, but the area between my lungs, in the lymph nodes, seems to be under attack now (not in my lungs, or attached to my lungs, just between them).

We don't have a plan right now other than we'll be heading to Houston sometime soon to get a consultation at M.D. Anderson (Med school there). They will work out a treatment plan and maybe run some tests and then we'll come back here and get started.

This is quite literally some of the worst news I could have anticipated. There is only one thing that could make it worse, and I'm getting an MRI in the next few days to confirm that or not.

THURSDAY, SEPTEMBER 10, 2009

Disappointed

MY GOAL WITH THIS BLOG IS to be real with you about who I am, and the struggles that I am going through. This isn't simply a "cancer update" thing, this is a "how is Ben really doing" thing. This is for several reasons:

1. So you can better know how to help me through this, and
2. So you don't get some illusion about who I am.

With those things in mind I wanted to share what I felt yesterday: I was disappointed with God. I felt like with all the prayer support and encouragement that, while I had to endure something scary, that the doctors were going to pass on a strange, but clean, bill of health.

That wasn't the case.

I found myself asking where God was. Why didn't He show up to dazzle the medical staff? Granted I had some personal motives for wanting this, but I felt like I had done what God said to do and to ask Him for things I wanted (and several hundred other people helped). However, God said no.

And I was disappointed. People sent me SO many promises of God that they were praying for me and I prayed as well, but God said no. I don't know what He is doing in my life, or why, but this isn't just a re-occurrence of my old cancer. This is a more rare form of it. It typically doesn't travel outside the abdomen, and here it is between my lungs. Double rare.

To survive this thing once was God, to survive this thing twice is going to require Him to save me again. From a strictly numbers point of view I am completely screwed. But God doesn't work in percentages (John Piper, "Don't Waste Your Cancer") and so I have to believe, despite my disappointment yesterday, that God (you know, the creator of everything and the guy who is omni-everything) knows what He is doing. I have literally no clue, and it is scary.

I can freak out about this, but that really doesn't change the fact that I have it. (However my subconscious mind seems to be doing a pretty good job of freaking out.) So what I will do, despite the fact that things didn't turn out as I had hoped/ prayed/ planned, I will continue to cling to my belief that God:

1. Has my best in mind,
2. Has a plan that will not only benefit me, but everyone around me, and
3. God hasn't abandoned me.

I guess the only thing to do at this point is hang on, fight, and see what happens next.

SATURDAY, SEPTEMBER 12, 2009

To live, to die

SOMETHING I TOLD A FRIEND of mine yesterday that I have been thinking more about lately is the verse in Philippians in the Bible where it says, "To live is Christ, to die is gain." – Philippians 1:21

It's kind of one of those verses that I mentally understood. Ok, yes, to live on the earth is to live for Christ and dying I get to go to heaven. Ok, I understand that in my head. I still don't WANT to die though!

More recently though I have come to understand that verse perhaps at more of a "heart" level. My life on this earth is a mostly scary, intimidating, and disappointing thing. No matter how many times I beat cancer, the fear of it coming back will ALWAYS hang over my head. No matter what I think the outcome should be, there is ALWAYS the fact that God might have different plans for me. No matter how much I think I might want something and think that it will change/ fulfill something in my life, odds are good that once I get it I'll be disappointed in some way with it.

I think some of it too probably has to do with a book I am in the process of trying to read about Heaven, and quite honestly that has changed how I think about the life after this one ("Heaven" by Randy Alcorn. The book should be sub-titled: "If you think the Bible doesn't say anything about Heaven, think again").

I think the real "fear" part comes in the passing from one to the other. However I don't think babies like being born either. That's I guess the last time I passed from one state to another. No one asked my opinion then either.

I'm not writing this to let you know I'm going

to cash my chips in early. Nope. As long as I have the strength to fight this (and probably beyond) I will fight for my life. I'm just saying that I don't think I am as afraid of the outcome as maybe I was last time. (O death where is your sting? 1 Corinthians 15:55)

SATURDAY, SEPTEMBER 26, 2009

The Christian Bait and Switch

WHEN YOU ARE A NON-CHRISTIAN, Christians will make the effort to invite you to things or they will try to tell you about God. All this is good and worthwhile, in fact God calls us to tell the world about Him. (Probably not as aggressively as some people in history have pursued it)

The point is that they will tell you that God is love, and that He died for your sins, you will most likely hear John 3:16, Romans 3:23, Romans 6:23, and Romans 5:8. The gist: You've sinned just by being alive, and sin leads to death, however there is an out! This is where the love of God comes in and they will tell you about how Great God is. And while they aren't lying, these people will most likely leave out something that I think is very important to tell you about before you accept Christ.

Yes: God forgives the things you have done, and He loves us beyond what we can comprehend.

However: The thing you will not be told when all this is being spelled out is that if you let God into your life: Your. Life. Is. Over.

Plans for the future? Yeah, you can plan, but that is kind of the trade-off. God saves you from your sin and you get to go to Heaven, but you know what? He has control of your life now. You can plan whatever you like, but odds are very good that He will use you someday to influence His world.

You know what? When He calls, odds are very good that it will interfere with your plans. "What? Why, God, are you sending me to Africa?", "Why are you sending me to Colorado?", "Why did I lose my job?", "Why did I lose my friend/ child/ sibling/ parent?"

There are a hundred things that can happen to steer us in a new direction. BUT, all of them are going to be something YOU never planned. To follow Jesus, really and honestly, IS salvation. To follow Christ on this Earth IS death to your own plans. This is the little detail that my fellow North Americans don't often reveal. I think in other places of the world they know this. The cost is evident.

So where does that leave us? Faith. I now have to believe that because I put my trust in Him, that He is going to take care of me, watch out for me, and have my best in mind. Even though I can tell you, especially now as cough all over my keyboard because my lymph nodes are swelling and pushing on my lungs, that you will wonder sometimes if what God is doing with you is for "your best."

But maybe it's not just about here and now. Maybe you and I have something beyond this life. What if this is just the minute staging ground for something much bigger, that will last hundreds of time longer. What if the difference was Heaven and Hell? I don't need to spell out to you what those are, odds are good you've heard it.

This life is hard. The past couple years have taught me this. The other day I was thinking about no pain, fear, or sorrow in Heaven and I got excited. I can't say how long I have here. I could have years and years left to "recount the deeds of the Lord" (Psalms 118:17) or maybe my time is up sometime in the next year. I don't know. I don't know at this point that it matters.

If I live, I have many exciting things I want to do: I'd love to have children, I'd like to see more of the world, I'd like to get OC off of Lotus Notes. God knows all this. I'm not surprising Him with this information. But here is the thing that is different about my life: I gave it to God and I let Him choose now what is best for me.

What else can I say? That is the choice. Follow God, and trust He knows what He is doing. Or don't. My Hope is in God at this point. I'm trying to hope extravagantly that what my God has in store for me is "beyond what [I] could ask or imagine." (Ephesians 3:20)

SUNDAY, SEPTEMBER 27, 2009

From Upstairs

"I WILL GIVE YOU THE TREASURES of darkness and the hoards in secret places, that you may know that it is I, the LORD, the God of Israel, who call you by your name."

— Isaiah 45:3 (ESV)

From the "I think God is trying to tell me something" department comes this little jewel: Isaiah 45:3. On Friday I was wandering the office checking on people as I will do from time to time and I dropped in on Ralph, OC's pastor/ Chaplain/ all around great guy, and we chatted for a bit. Towards the end he stopped me and said his wife had reminded him of a verse that he thought I could use right about now. He brought up and read Isaiah 45:3. Not what you would call a common verse, or something that someone hands people in times of distress. But I liked it and it spoke to me.

Then that afternoon the board called me in and prayed for me. And one of the board members' wives prayed Isaiah 45:3 over me (well, she said the verse, she didn't reference it, but I knew where it was from from earlier that day). Two times in one day someone references an obscure verse in Isaiah? Ok Lord, I'm listening.

This is a great verse for several reasons:

1. It mentions treasures of darkness. There are things hidden in darkness, in trials, and in pain that cannot be gotten without venturing down into those depths. God is saying that there is purpose to going there.

2. The second part of that verse gives me chills: "that you may know that it is I, the LORD, the God of Israel, who call you by your name." Wow. God telling me, "I know you, I can see you there in the darkness, and I am calling you out by your name." This isn't like, "Hey, you, is someone in there?" No. This is God saying, "Ben, I see you there in your troubles and pain, and there is something down there for you. But I can still see you. You are not lost to me and you will be rescued." (I of course do not know in what form that rescue will take, but God has not only my back, but my front and my sides as well.)

OCTOBER, COLORADO SPRINGS

TUESDAY, OCTOBER 6, 2009

A tablespoon of hope

WELL, I HAVE TO ADMIT I WAS kind of expecting to hear something not very easy to handle this morning, but I wasn't sure. I remained hopeful, but still. Waiting is stressful.

The doctor came in and pulled up the PET scans. He told us after he had seen what my platelets were at last week he had expected to see the cancer in my bones as well as the other places. Good news on that front: There are only 4 tumors. Three under my sternum (smallish) and then a fairly large one around my trachea and behind my heart. Which makes it very, very difficult to operate on.

However, the good news is that there are only 4, and they are in the same place that we thought they would be in. There wasn't anything hidden somewhere else (like inside my bones).

Some additional good news is that the doctor is going to try a lighter chemo regime on me as well. I'll get two rounds of this type of chemo and come back here for more scans and a prognosis.

The good news about this "new" type of chemo is it's "outpatient" which means I don't need to spend days and nights in the hospital getting this stuff pumped into my body. I get to go in and spend about 3 hours a day getting the stuff pumped into me and then I go home. Which is very much nicer than staying in the hospital for 120 hours straight.

So, after 2 rounds of this (about 6 weeks) I will come back here for scans and what-not. I think the thing that makes me excited about this is that the doctor was very optimistic. Last week when we met with him he pretty much told me 2 to 3 years is what I could expect life-span wise. This time he told me that if the cancer responds to the chemo he can actually see me kicking this permanently.

FRIDAY, OCTOBER 23, 2009

I hate this week

HERE IT IS ON A FRIDAY NIGHT and it pretty much puts an end to one of the worst weeks I have had in years. Chemo destroyed my week. If it wasn't one thing it was another. Today it was that my mouth was burning so badly I couldn't eat or drink anything without it feeling like I was swallowing acid. So then nurse gave me some pain killer, which made the pain go away. I happily ate for the first time in about 16 hours and then a few hours later threw it all up again because the pain killer made me queasy.

Now I am taking like 3 or 4 different pills/ liquids, to make my mouth better, or to combat nausea, or to make me nauseous (oral chemo), and my mouth still hurts too much to drink or eat anything.

I've lost 5 pounds this week. And I am frustrated to the point of tears. I really hate my life right now.

2010

JANUARY, COLORADO SPRINGS

MONDAY, JANUARY 4, 2010

Anytime any reason

I WAS READING **PHILIPPIANS 1** this morning because I grabbed my Bible and randomly flipped it open, mainly because my attitude about this week was horrible and it hadn't even started yet. I was thinking I needed to refocus and God really helped me out. Philippians 1:18-26 is what I came across this morning. It contains the verse I have quoted before: "To live is Christ, die gain." -Philippians 1:21

It reminded me (the whole section 18 - 26) that I currently serve here by the grace of God.

Living is to benefit you all, and if God sees fit to end my life, anytime for any reason, then you all will benefit more from that than my life. It's a hard reality to live with. I'm here for you, and when I can do more good dead God will make it happen. But I guess that is the case with any of us... whether we realize that or not.

That helped my attitude a bit this morning. A bit of humble pie from Philippians.

SUNDAY, JANUARY 10, 2010

Happy birthday to me

THE INFUSION CENTER THIS morning had some cake, ice cream, vomit bags, and a shot for me. Not how I ever imagined spending the start to my 28th year, but the support has been excellent (BTW I made it to 28!!).

TUESDAY, JANUARY 12, 2010

Tired

I AM SO TIRED. Tired of just about everything. I am especially tired of pulling myself out of the hole that is chemo every 2-3 weeks. 9 to 10 more months of this? Where can I get off? Maybe next time they can put me into a drug induced coma for 8 days following chemo just to get it over with.

I went downstairs to find lunch and barely had enough energy to get myself upstairs again. Plus trying to keep myself hydrated and find something my body thinks is edible is taking a lot of energy. I need calories because 133 pounds is not a safe weight to be at.

Maybe I can work out a deal with a pizza place to deliver pizza at lunchtime every day. My guess is my body probably wouldn't like that too much either.

I'm sorry, I am really frustrated and there isn't really anything I can do about it.

SUNDAY, JANUARY 24, 2010

Round... 5?

I THINK WE'RE ABOUT TO HIT round 5 here of chemo. Which means I have spent 5 weeks in the infusion center, and about 13 weeks recovering from my 5 weeks in the infusion center.

I'm tired. Mentally I think I am prepared for another week of this. I'm not sure about physically. I felt like recovery this time took longer, but I also felt like when I had recovered (Thursday, Friday, and Saturday) that I was more recovered than some of the other times. I don't know that that is a good thing or not. I'm pretty sure I don't want my body (and the cancer) getting used to this chemo at all.

So, my treatment is at 9:30 tomorrow morning and I would appreciate prayer for its effectiveness as well as the recovery (this seems strange, I am asking that the chemo waste parts of my body and yet at the same time asking that it not work as hard on my body so I can recover faster. I think if I had my choice of the two I'd go for the "waste my body" which equals "kill cancer").

FEBRUARY, COLORADO SPRINGS and HOUSTON

WEDNESDAY, FEBRUARY 3, 2010

So tired

I HAVE BEEN SLEEPING THROUGH the night but my body seems to be working harder than usual to fix itself, and it is leaving me insanely drained. I seriously haven't been in this much prolonged pain since I had shingles at the end of my last bout with this cancer.

They gave me some kind of liquid painkiller that does a pretty good job of taking away the pain, but one of the side effects (besides tasting like pineapple soap) seems to be appetite suppressant and at my last weigh in I was a solid 130lbs. Which is I believe the lowest point I was at last time I had a run in with DSCRT.

I BADLY need to gain weight and as much as I would like to do it by eating everything fatty and generally bad for me (pizza 3 times a week wouldn't be bad for me would it? I mean, what if it was veggie pizza?) I really feel like I should at least attempt some pretty healthy eating, being as no one really knows what causes this cancer, it sure wouldn't hurt to hit my body with just about everything healthy I can find.

I have to confess that it's weeks like this that my battle seems too much to bear. It's hard living and makes me so tired. Especially when I spend pretty much all day in bed without doing a whole lot. I am very glad for my laptop which becomes a kind of portal to outside.

FRIDAY, FEBRUARY 5, 2010

What's next?

I AM TIRED OF BEING TIRED as often as I am. If I had planned things I would have been at OC today helping with a domain migration that has been a year plus in the planning. But today I am at home completely worn out from low potassium and magnesium counts. My pain level hasn't disappeared, but it has gone down to a level that I can easily ignore most of the time.

But I find myself wondering, as I have planned

none of this cancer stuff, and it looks like I'm going to be in this battle for another 9 months at least, I wonder what's next? I pray daily that God will make this cancer disappear.

Here we are in February, with looking at something like October before chemo is over. I am standing at the foothills with what I have gone through already and I am looking up towards the peak and I do not know if I will see the summit. And then when I get there are there more mountains behind? Will I ever kick this? My strength is not sufficient to hold me out for more than a couple years of this. I must rely on God's strength for my solutions, but I don't know how much of this, how long, I want to battle this.

This last week was a lot to handle, and I am torn down.

WEDNESDAY, FEBRUARY 17, 2010

Today's the day

OK, TODAY'S THE DAY. We find out if the chemo has been having any more effect on these crazy tumors. I'm not going to lie: these meetings with the doctor are probably some of the scariest things that happen in my life. I have NO idea what he is going to say when he comes in. It could range from "wow great news!" to "Well it's not responding like I'd like" to "Bad news, there has been a massive cell reproduction."

I mean I walk in there (and wait forever) and I don't know what the rundown is going to be until he sits down and starts talking. Yes he said some hopeful things last time, but this cancer stuff (excuse me) is a bitch and sometimes the chemo works, and sometimes it doesn't.

I am going to go spend some time with God. He's gotten me this far (through this once already when it was 3 times harder at least). We'll see what He has to say.

P.S. I am shaking in my boots over this meeting. The chemo I am currently on is still Plan A. We still have B and C to go if this is failing.

Mountains

I WAS JUST SINGING SOME Rich Mullins songs to myself. When I sang, "Hold me Jesus" there is a line that made me pause and think: "Sometimes this life just don't make sense at all, when the mountains look so big, and my faith just seems so small."

I got to thinking about what big mountains look like. I stare up at Pike's Peak almost every day. That mountain looks like one you can't climb. Then I remembered something I tell a lot of people: Zebulon Pike, one of the old founders of Colorado Springs, looked at the mountain and said, "I don't think it'll ever be climbed." To which I laughingly add, "And now there is a gift shop at the top!" (And at least 3 different ways to get to the top: train, car or hike.)

So this got me thinking about the mountain in front of me. Like living in Colorado Springs, the mountain looks big, but we are also already at 6500 feet. Like me, I've already been up part of this mountain range before. This trek before me looks impossible... but who knows, someday there might be a gift shop at the top, or at least a flag, to mark that and tell the story of how I got to the top of my mountain.

We go in hopeful and victorious.

Stable

WELL, WORD FROM THE DOC is that the tumors are stable. They haven't changed much/ at all from the last time. But I guess "stable" is better than "larger".

We got a lot of information but I really don't have the emotional fortitude to put all that down at the moment.

We're a little disappointed, but this is where we're at now.

THURSDAY, FEBRUARY 18, 2010

Time-zones

IT'S 4:30AM HERE IN Houston. I don't know why 3am is when I wake up, but it is. I am very worn out. Wish I wasn't up.

The doctor yesterday told me at this point the cancer is stable. At the same time kind of crushing some hopes in the process. He said that there is too much cancer by my heart and trachea that he is afraid my heart would get too much radiation/ it would burn up my throat.

He also said that surgery would most likely be life threatening (though he said there was a guy here in town who would do a routine where he REMOVES my heart, clears it off and the surrounding area, and puts it back. Can't imagine recovery from that is easy). And then surgery on my trachea could/would damage it permanently.

So it looks like this chemo and/or stronger chemo is the way it's going to go. Though there are some experimental treatments I am not sure if my platelets would stay high enough for me to get in and stay in one of those. My platelets already tend to trend low.

I continue to ask God what He is doing, but I don't really get the answers I am looking for so much. "Making you stronger" and "Impacting other people's lives" are generally what I hear. I have yet to hear, "Making you a medical wonderland of mysteriously healed mega rare cancers." (Not like that isn't still an option, and it is very much still a hope.)

We were seeing a therapist awhile back and something he said stuck with me. He said that with God in our lives there is very seldom one answer to "why." Which I guess is something I understand.

I guess sometimes I just don't understand as it seems to me that God gave me a great mind for technology and how it works and how I can help further His kingdom with it. And in MY mind that would be a more effective use of my life. However, that's not what I am doing right now. And honestly, I don't understand. I don't have the answers I want. I have some answers, but not so much the ones I really want... but I guess that is why they call it faith, huh? Why would I trust that God knows what He is doing if I had all the answers? I love technology and helping people. God also knows the other desires of my heart and things I want to do. The mountain is steep, but I hope to put a gift shop up there.

MARCH, COLORADO SPRINGS

Some foreshadowing: Please remember the following passage in order to note the irony of what happens later. God certainly has a sense of humor.

SUNDAY, MARCH 7, 2010

Haven't moved

Hey Folks, I have heard from several different sources that some of you think we have moved to Texas. No offense to the Texan readers out there, BUT, there is seriously no chance I would ever move to Texas of my own free will. (Which probably amounts to me just saying something like, "Send me anywhere Lord, just don't send me to ________________ (country)!" and ending up in

__________ (country).

We make semi frequent trips down there to see my "expert" in my cancer, Dr. Ludwig, but that is about the only moving we will do in that direction. Colorado might get cold, but at least I see the sun. Summers here have been AMAZINGLY nice. We could use a touch more rain in the spring, but other than that, I like this place a lot.

TUESDAY, MARCH 9, 2010

Contention

"**God has said, 'Never will I leave you;** never will I forsake you.' So we say with confidence, 'The Lord is my helper; I will not be afraid. What can man do to me?'"

— Hebrews 13:5-6

Of all the things I forget and need to be reminded of most often it is the above two lines: "Never will I leave you; never will I forsake you." So many times I sit here and think that my life is doomed because I haven't petitioned God enough to heal me. As if I need to be the little kid: "Dad? Dad? Hey Dad? Daaaad! Dad? Are you listening Dad? Dad! Look at me Dad! Look what I can do Dad! Dad?"

And what does that verse say? That verse says that God already knows. I don't need to keep thinking that if I don't mention healing me that

God is going to forget to do it, or it's not going to happen. What, I'll die and get to Heaven and God will be like, "Whoops, what are you doing here?"

Not, of course, that we are supposed to stop asking God for things. I just think about my attitude when I have been out of it for a week or more and I am thinking I am somehow behind now.

This also puts God in a much more loving light. Yes, God is love, but if you imagine that you have to keep trying to get His attention out of several BILLION people you can't really believe there is much love there. Or if you think you are hiding in billions of people and God doesn't notice you. But if He will never leave us or forsake us, it's like those billions of people disappear and it's me and God. Like He's sitting right here on the couch with me. It's not a contest between me and billions of other people for His attention. It's me and God.

TUESDAY, MARCH 23, 2010

Valdez

As I was getting my final and most dangerous chemo of the day yesterday a new part, a part that is supposed to keep everyone safer, popped off from the backpressure and suddenly the tube was swinging freely back and forth as the pump cranked out chemo. Only it wasn't going into me, it was going on the floor, on the chair, on the pump. My nurse rapidly shut it down but still the cleanup was CRAZY.

She put on a special hat, goggles, two pairs of gloves, an extra gown, and booties for her shoes. My blanket was wrapped in a biohazard bag and I had to take it home and wash it twice.

Anyway, she got all dressed up in this gear to protect her and here I was sitting there without any protection. I was like, "Great, and THIS is what you are pumping into my insides? Don't I get any protection?"

Her response, "Well, you already have cancer."

"Great... thanks Anne, thanks."

My first chemo spill, and humorously enough it came from a safety device. I'm glad my nurses have a sense of humor. It would make this all a lot more difficult.

WEDNESDAY, MARCH 24, 2010

A silver lining

AS MUCH AS I WOULD RATHER be doing almost ANYTHING other than going through chemo and having to deal with it I can sometimes see the silver lining to it, or something that probably would not have happened had I been around and doing my job. I would say at OC the almost a year I spent there was as a dreamer of where the IT could go, and then setting up a plan and trying to get it rolling. I was a catalyst to help people see clearly where they were at with technology, and where they could go with current technology to make information accessible to EVERYONE on the field.

Anyway, one thing I have seen from my being gone and not being there to spearhead and or lead the whole project(s) myself has been a lot bigger buy-in from various departments and people. Instead of me holding the reins to some technology changes, it has become a bigger project that has gone much further than I could have planned it to go. It's kind of exciting in some ways, it still very much makes me want to be there, and helping and tossing in my two bits, but God has me on the outside right now. I want to be back in some kind of IT role again someday, and really hope the passion, as well as the skills, that God has given me isn't to end up short lived. But that is His choice, and frankly there are probably 50% of my days these days, if not more, where I find myself wondering if Heaven needs an IT guy. Or maybe an explorer, or a writer. This isn't easy, and it's not getting easier.

APRIL, COLORADO SPRINGS

FRIDAY, APRIL 9, 2010

Dear Lord

DEAR LORD,

This morning I am nervous. I am concerned about what the doctor is going to say this afternoon. My nervousness stems from the vast difference in what my future could be after this afternoon. There is SO much you know Lord, and yet so much I do not. Am I weak in faith for being worried or nervous about what I might hear this afternoon?

Forgive me for my doubt Lord, but I need your strength to make it day to day, both physically and mentally. I seriously cannot do this, the cancer and the "cure" both drain me.

Please heal me, because only you can Lord. You have given me so many talents and dreams, please do not let these go unused. Further my skills and my dreams for the future, give me hope and help me shine brightly for You. You know my future Lord, and I do not, but I ask for healing, and for an amazing story I can someday tell everyone about your healing grace.

Thank you for the many blessings in my life: my wife, a place to live, health insurance, family, friends, co-workers who care, a job, technology (medical and otherwise), and so many other things. Thank you.

The scan Ben saw later that day didn't show much change. That weekend, Ben and Lisa tried to spend the night in a Denver hotel, but Ben ended up going to the ER with gallstones instead. He had his gallbladder removed laparoscopically on April 15th, continuing his trend of having unnecessary organs removed.

WEDNESDAY, APRIL 28, 2010

A day in the life

HERE IS A BIT OF A WALK down on what my day looks like from up-time to back-to-bed time. Not sure how much "fun" this is, but you mind find it a bit interesting.

3:00am Wake up with things that chemo likes to keep you awake for.

4:50 Fall back asleep

7:27 Get up and get ready for my day.

7:55 Lisa talking about lunch makes me throw up.

8:05 Drive to hospital

8:35 Arrive at infusion center, said, "Hey" to all the nurses.

8:40 Get weighed and vitals checked out. Appears I am alive.

8:45 Talk to nurse about me and gallbladders.

8:50 Get hooked up to the pump, start getting the anti-nausea drugs.

9:05 Start writing day in the life of chemo. Waiting for painkiller and chemo.

9:10 Nurse comes over and says we're waiting for meds. I start re-reading Wired from yesterday. Such a solid mag.

9:30 Chat with my nurse about chemo drug history as she gives me some Ativan and Dilaudid for the strange pain/feeling of chemo burning through my body. Possibly feeling a bit tired. No chemo yet. Feeling sleepy.

9:45 First round of chemo starts - 60

minutes until the next one. Painkiller did a great job of hiding the strange pain. Back to Wired.

10:55 Hooked up to last chemo. Will take 90 minutes. Pretty tired we'll see what happens.

12:30 Rolls around and they unhook me

12:35 I am picked up by a patron from church

1:00 Get home and nap most of the day.

5:30 Dinner. Hiccupping starts.

5:35 Watch some TV with Lisa. Can't stop hiccuping.

8:00 Getting close to bedtime.

That is roughly what my day looked like. The painkiller really helps keep me a bit tired and so I can't feel the strange effects of the chemo.

JUNE, COLORADO SPRINGS and HOUSTON

WEDNESDAY, JUNE 9, 2010

90-10

UNFORTUNATELY, AFTER TWO HOURS in the Dr.'s office, things didn't quite go as well as I had hoped. 90 percent of my tumors are "stable" and the other 10 percent seems to be growing. bleh. So my chemo regime is going to be changing. They are going to try and get me into a trial drug thing. If I can't do that then I will go to a higher dose of chemo and radiation.

Not too excited about any of this, I was hoping to get some results so I could plan a vacation but that didn't happen. Oh well, I guess I'll have to keep going about this whole thing day by day like I was before.

MONDAY, JUNE 14, 2010

Didn't we just...

DESPITE THE FACT THAT we were JUST in Houston, we are in fact headed right back. That's right, a week from today I will be meeting with the doctor who might be giving me the new treatments.

The people who have seen the study have all had very positive things to say about it. I have to confess if it is half of what it's supposed to be then it'll be far better than any chemo I've had to date.

TUESDAY, JUNE 22, 2010

Returned

DOCTOR'S VISIT WENT PRETTY WELL. They all seemed pretty nice and very "international" (people from all over the world seem to be working there). It sounds like I will probably get into the study, but the day we were there (Monday) one of the participants had been admitted to the hospital. If his admission had anything to do with the drugs, then they can't accept new people, but the doctor assumed it was because of his "sickness" that he went into the hospital, not the drugs. So we have to wait until the end of the week or so to get information on if I am in or not.

IF I get into the study I am looking at one

treatment of two kinds of drugs once a week for two months as "two rounds". Then they evaluate me and see how everything is going. I will be the sixth person in this trial if I get in. Surprisingly enough they have another person already in the study who has the same type of cancer that I have (!!!) and the doctor was telling us that after "two rounds" the cancer has shown a complete shutdown. Which is really exciting. However I am a different person than them, and I have yet to get into the study.

I'll be poking around housing situations in Houston as well, and trying to figure out what to do with our place here too. The study is supposed to go on "indefinitely," so while we could at least schedule two months at first I am really not sure what we are looking at here. I really am not a fan of moving to Houston on a more permanent basis. (Sorry friends who live in Houston now or did at some point. Lisa and I are not big fans of heat.)

WEDNESDAY, JUNE 23, 2010

Angry Reindeer Study

WHAT YOU SEE HERE BELOW is what greeted us on the white board in the exam room we waited in. If we had been dropped in there and seen nurses and doctors and then been ushered out, we never would have seen what this medical study was really about. BUT leave the Morrells in a room, by themselves, for long enough and the truth will come out! I'll endeavor to explain what you are seeing here in the most non-scientific way possible so that you can understand what it looks like I am going to go through for this study.

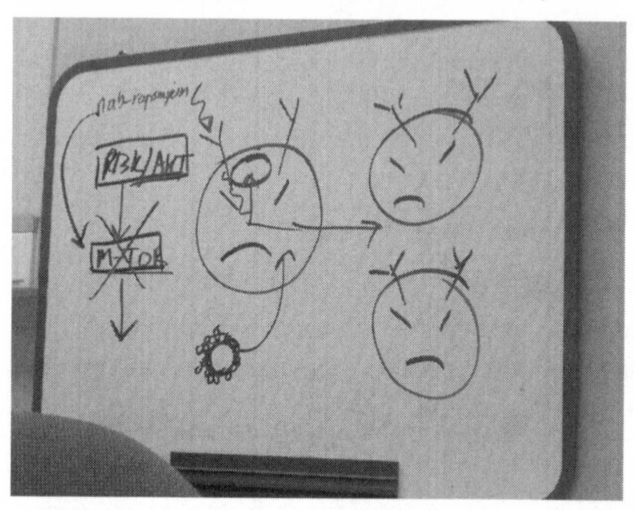

"Rangifer tarandus" (Reindeer, or Caribou as they are called) don't like cancer. Most of the time, however, reindeer are far too apathetic to care about rapidly dividing crazy cells in other creatures' bodies. It has been discovered that if you can work them up, get them good and angry, that they cure cancer.

You'll see on the board that there is a certain amount of risk involved with getting a reindeer angry enough to cure cancer. The little squiggly round thing below the fully grown male reindeer in the picture is what is often referred to in medical circles as the "irritant." In this study they are using steel wool and duct-tape applied to the forehead of the reindeer.

The reindeer, when angered sufficiently, knock the study participant to the ground and, much like a faith healer in a charismatic church, heals the cancer patient. It is unknown at this time what it is about the angry reindeer that prompts this response in cancer. Maybe like the Elephant and the Mouse they are just natural enemies, but the effect only seems to work when the animal is angered. Apathetic (or the "meh" state as referred to in the study) reindeer seem to have no effect. At this time the study sample is small, in both reindeer used and humans.

It's exciting to be at the cutting edge of medical technology.

SATURDAY, JUNE 26, 2010

No word yet

LAST WEEK CAME AND WENT and no word from "the Anderson" (I think it's actually shorter to just type MD Anderson than giving it a nickname like that. Hmmm) on my trial. My guess is that they probably know BUT were busy and didn't get around to picking up the phone. Hopefully I'll hear something early next week. I guess we'll bug them if we don't hear anything on Monday. We gotta know if we are moving or not.

I have to admit the alternative (staying

here and getting a stronger dose of chemo and radiation) does not thrill me at all. HOWEVER, God is in control (thankfully) and not me. Which means He knows what is going to be best for me long (and short) term. I know which way I would like things to go, though. I'd kind of like to try the "Remarkable Results for Your Type of Cancer" route.

SUNDAY, JUNE 27, 2010

Iron[y/ic]

I'VE BEEN THINKING ABOUT it and it's funny. (What is "it"? you ask) "It" is my treatments and, quite frankly, they aren't funny, but it's a kind of "funny" twist. I have to move to Houston to get treatments that will make me feel better, and not affect me as hard as the chemo I have been having, and odds are good I will feel good enough to work. However, I will be in Houston, and out of reach of my job except for what I can manage to do remotely (which I am hoping is a lot).

On the flip side, if I stay here and do chemo and radiation then I am faced with being too sick to work. It's a "funny" twist.

Part of this that makes the choices as "funny" as they are is that part of my goal when taking the job I currently have was to de-centralize IT for the company so it didn't matter if you were in Colorado Springs, Singapore, or Gamrie so long as you had an Internet connection. Granted any office of a certain size is going to need an actual IT person to do network, desktop, and general software troubleshooting, but the system should be set up so that as long as there is an Internet connection help can be requested at any time and the connection should be almost instant, or at least within 24 hours.

As we are spread all over the globe I see no reason why our IT infrastructure shouldn't be as well. Ooo, gotta be careful, getting excited there. You're going to get a whole novel sized paragraph on this if I don't stop now. Anyway, that is some of the excitement I feel like I have been missing out on while being sick. This is why I see my (potential) move to Houston as a potentially good thing right now. Not only for the medical reasons, but for seeing what we can make happen remotely.

MONDAY, JUNE 28, 2010

Houston! (Again, again)

THREE ROAD TRIPS TO HOUSTON in a month's time. We're putting as many miles on the car in one month as we would normally do in six months. The upside would be that we are getting to know Texas really well.

Aaaand, more news, we are temporarily moving to Houston! I made it into the clinical trial and being as treatments are once a week for at least two months we are going to move to Houston during that time to make that happen (flying once a week would not be a good thing). We leave next Wednesday!

We have a place in Houston lined up already. Praise God for contacts of contacts. We are looking for a potential renter of our place here in Colorado Springs right now.

Wow, I've got so much stuff going through my head right now I'm not even sure what to blog about. More info later.

JULY, HOUSTON

THURSDAY, JULY 1, 2010

Houston Hides

IT'S KIND OF FUNNY. You Houston folks, or people who have family in Houston, really come out of the woodwork when the "chips" are down (and for that we are grateful). We've already had more dinner invites, and church invites, than the first three months of living here in Colorado Springs. The weather might be nicer here, but so far Houston has the more welcoming group of people (a good amount of whom we have yet to actually meet in person).

FRIDAY, JULY 2, 2010

Another Post about H-town

I WAS TRYING TO GET TO SLEEP tonight and our 85+ degree room was preventing that so I was growing introspective and thought I would turn that into a blog post.

Everyone who has seriously considered missions in their Christian life has at one point or another probably said something like, "Use me Lord... but please don't send me to ____________" (the running joke would be something like "Africa" or "Mexico").

I realized tonight that Houston is our Africa. I would say that Colorado Springs is a pretty cushy assignment and there is little here to really complain about. Houston... well, I think after our first visit there (oncologist and planes notwithstanding) we were pretty sure we didn't want to spend much more time there. Send us anywhere God, just don't send us to Houston. And, much like the punch line to the "Don't send me to Africa or Mexico" joke, we'll be ending up there.

In some ways I am very excited about the prospects of this trial (highly positive effects with minimal side effects) I can't help but have a feeling though that there is more to this temporary move than just trying more medication for me. From my experience, God never really seems to deal in singular things. There is no ONE "Why did I get sick?" There is no singular answer to the question, "Why did we move to Colorado?"

While I am sure you and I would like AN answer, the workings of God on our lives are many tiered. Some we will be able to see, and many we cannot. I know that is running into trite territory, but it's true. I think though that as difficult as that is to swallow sometimes, it adds depth to our lives.

I guess I find myself awake tonight marveling at the complexity of God in my life.

FRIDAY, JULY 9, 2010

We have arrived!

I ENDED UP DRIVING OVER FIVE hours the first day from Colorado Springs to Amarillo and then ALL day from Amarillo to Fort Worth. I wimped out and didn't drive at all today. I am glad we only packed what we could fit into the, errr, Fit. If we had rented a U-Haul then we would have taken more stuff, and more stuff would have meant more to unpack, which I would have been almost worthless with.

As it was I kind of helped move some stuff around when we got here, but not a huge amount. Lisa, in typical Lisa fashion, has almost everything unpacked already. It's a nice place that we are staying. We haven't done the drive to the medical center yet, so we'll see how that goes.

Speaking of medical center (ooo, check out

that segway) I have appointments set up for all next week. Monday is "test day," where I get blood taken out of me, and more radiation put into me than most normal people get in a year... or two (the directions specifically say to avoid pregnant women and young children under 5 for at least 24 hours after because of my "hotness" {radioactivity that is}).

The next day I have a meeting with a doctor in the afternoon. Then on Wednesday they are most likely going to be starting my treatment. At 5pm. I guess with all the people they have getting treatments around here it's a pretty busy place. Which means I'll probably be at the hospital from 5pm-ish to 9 or later on Wednesday. BUT it does sound like I am starting on Wednesday, no matter how late it seems. So you and I will get to see how the side effects go the rest of the week.

MONDAY, JULY 12, 2010

The Pokings!

OH THE POKINGS! While the blood drawer was effective at what she was doing, it also felt like she ran the needle halfway through my arm to do it. We shall see what that bruise looks like. Let me back up a bit here (record being slid backwards quickly under the needle sound).

Last night Google informed me it would take an hour and a half in traffic from our current location to get to MD Anderson. This thrilled me not at all, but Lisa and I were up at 5:30am just to make that 6:15am leave time. We were out the door by 6:30am and at the hospital by 7am. Either we were out too early for the traffic thing to hit, or we were going the other way (I vote for the early part, as I don't think there IS "the other way" in Houston).

That was when I got poked the first time, then I got radiation shot at me for a bit (chest x-ray), then sat around for an hour while I waited to spend 30 seconds getting an EKG. Then we waited some more for the PET scan time, and got poked (three more times) there. I, however, got a nice little nap while waiting for those "nuclear" sugars to take effect.

Then it was back in the tube for 18 minutes of whirring and clicking and, most importantly, more radiation. I like how they say to avoid pregnant ladies, small children, and the elderly for 24 hours after that scan (and then send you home past all the pregnant ladies, small children, and elderly). Lots of stuff to find funny here.

Lisa is doing a bang-up job getting us settled. You'd almost never know we brought a whole car full of stuff with us. Speaking of Lisa, did you know that Friday is our 5 YEAR anniversary? That's right, as of this Friday I will have been married to Lisa longer than I was in high school, longer than I have ever had a job for, and yes, LONGER than I have had cancer(though it feels longer sometimes).

Assuming, which is a lot for us these days, that we are both well on Friday, we're going out to lunch to celebrate. It's just like dinner, only it costs less and the sun is still out!

I am hoping this first five will be the part of our marriage we look back on and say, "Remember that year we spent in Houston those few months?" and "God brought us through cancer, He can bring us through this!" or even "If we can live in Houston, God can do anything!" (you'll notice the subtle dig on Houston there. It's all in good fun as this is the place we need to be right now. And as soon as it stops being the place we need to be we will no longer be here... Lord willing).

SATURDAY, JULY 24, 2010

Mortal Home

SEVERAL THINGS:

1. Since starting this cancer thing a few years back my mortality has continued to sit in front of me and tug on my shirt like a needy little three-year old. Sometimes when I think I have forgotten it for a while the strangest things will bring it roaring back. It seems to me like everyone knows they are going to die, but lives like they won't. It's kind of "funny" but only having chemo once a week really dials up the "oh my goodness something is wrong with

me!" thoughts. In some ways chemo on a daily basis is easier (mentally) than once a week. Daily, fighting cancer and balancing chemo side-effects is a job. Weekly, I have a "life" and cancer is something that is happening in/to my "life".

2. I've been evaluating the meaning of "home" lately with our moving from Seattle to COS and then to Houston. We left one "home" to do something and hopefully make a new one, but as we settled in cancer rose up again and we had to move again. I know Lisa still thinks of Seattle as home. And I guess that depends. If "home" is where you are the most known and know the most people then yes, Seattle would be "home". But we aren't home... and we can't go home easily.

I've been thinking about what "Home" is, especially combined with the ton of bricks that is the reminder that I will die. Add the pain of life and I honestly am starting to understand more and more the draw of making Heaven home. There are many upsides to this as I can see it: It doesn't matter where you go on Earth because my home isn't here, and homes here on earth can be destroyed, but no one is touching Heaven.

I don't know, just some thoughts this morning as I consider my life and the things that have "wrecked" what I thought it would be.

AUGUST, HOUSTON

SATURDAY, AUGUST 7, 2010

Friday with Friends

SOME MISSIONARIES FROM SPAIN who are part of OC are in town this next couple of weeks for some treatments at MD Anderson. We've been trying to get together for the past week or so but had little success, what with the waiting game that is MD Anderson. We finally both had open schedules and ended up spending more than four hours at lunch and then a coffee shop hanging out and talking.

We didn't really know each other before yesterday, we knew OF each other, but still, we made a quick connection over shared experiences and then it was just talking about the details.

I remember hearing a few sermons and such on "God's Appointments," being in places where you don't want to be but "luckily" or "crazily enough" you run into someone(s) who ends up needing you or you needing them (or both). I have been thinking lately that that is the case in my scenario, but I think it goes a little deeper than that. "God's Appointments" makes it seem just a level deep. What I have experienced, both this time with cancer and the last, is "God's Networking".

Case in point: We move to Colorado Springs, get involved with a great organization that allows me to do what I love (IT for Nonprofits) and connects me, casually, to more than 500 people all over the world. This connection enabled me to meet my temporary replacement while I was sick (Elliot) when we came to Houston the first time. They ended up moving to Colorado Springs to help with my job and Elliot ended up learning a whole lot about computers.

When we needed to move down here to Houston, Elliot hooked us up with their best friends here in town and we learned their parents needed someone to keep an eye on their house for a couple of months while they were out of town. "God's Networking."

I guess as much as I don't want to be going through cancer treatments, it has been interesting to look back and see the casual interactions and meetings I have with people are more than just a single point in time. What I do now has an effect, and while I might not have any idea what that might lead to in the future there is purpose here, there was purpose there. Again, it's not easy, but it is kind of exciting sometimes.

THURSDAY, AUGUST 19, 2010

The title of this post is a play on words. Ben had just started treatment at the Mays Clinic, which he found he vastly preferred over the main building of MD Anderson.

A-Mays-ing

I HAVE A **PET** SCAN COMING UP here in a few weeks (September 2nd) and we shall see what is going on inside of me. I had a dream last night that the scan came back "black" in the places where my cancer is at. Which means that the tumors weren't drawing any more sugar, which means complete tumor death. I don't know that I've ever had a dream about the status of my sickness in a dream before.

MONDAY, AUGUST 23, 2010

Raw

NOT EVERYTHING IS COMING UP sunshine and daisies here in Houston. There have been a lot of things as of late that I have been frustrated by, and chief among them is my lack of ability to swallow a pill. At first it wasn't too tricky, I'd do it first thing in the morning before I was awake and then that stopped working.

I end up choking on the thing almost every time now. Sometimes it goes down, other times it doesn't.

I think the thing that kind of scares me is that this isn't the only thing I have trouble with swallowing. Some foods don't really go down very easily anymore either. I had a massive coughing fit yesterday over some carrot. They said this could be a possible side effect of my tumors growing.

Another frustration is my blood sugar levels. It looks like I am slowly creeping into type two diabetes at the moment, which is going to mean way more self-sticking than I ever wanted to get into.

Then there is the upcoming scan. Combined with paragraph number one I'm kind of not sure if this trial is working or not. I feel better as a whole, but between the choking, the high cholesterol, and the blood sugar, I really don't know. I also haven't gained any weight since being here in Houston.

Then physical stuff aside there are the social aspects of this. Here we are in Houston, we don't know if we are staying or going, and we have friends in Colorado, we have friends and family all over Seattle. I'm stuck pretty close to Houston due to my treatments and my inability to fly.

I'm frustrated because I don't know what is going on here.

SEPTEMBER, HOUSTON

THURSDAY, SEPTEMBER 2, 2010

PET Scanning

IT LOOKS LIKE THE EARLY BIRD does indeed get the worm. And by worm I mean IV through which nuclear-powered sugars are pumped into one's body, and by bird I mean me. Lisa and I got up extra early this morning (5:30am for those keeping score at home) and battled medium traffic to MD Anderson where before my seat even had a chance to warm up and/or I had time to finish my survey about me (when was the last time you had a biopsy, chemo, surgery, do you have asthma, who is your favorite radioactively powered superhero, etc) I was whisked into the PET scan waiting area where they jabbed me with a needle, injected me with radioactive sugars, and then told me not to move for the next hour.

After my hour was up (well-done is how I like my insides) I was moved to the (freezing) cold room where the PET/CT scan tube is located. I then lay there for the next 18 minutes pretending the Arctic blast I was feeling was something I could ignore. They then dismissed me and told me to have a good day.

Our trip home took less than 25 minutes (reverse commute) and we were home before a lot of you Pacific time-zoners were even out of bed. I'll be waiting for next Wednesday to hear about how those scans look. I am hoping for less color, more darkness.

Thanks for the support everyone. Maybe by the end of next week we'll have some idea about staying here or being back in Colorado Springs.

WEDNESDAY, SEPTEMBER 8, 2010

Medical Update

IT LOOKS LIKE WE'LL CONTINUE to be in Houston for an unknown period of time.

The report/ scan from last week showed what the oncologist chose to label as "stable" tumors. This means that some (the ones nearest my heart) shrank, while others grew a bit. I guess the cutoff on me continuing this trial is if they show a growth of 20%... which, considering how much room is in my body, would be noticeable I think.

We'll continue this trial, and then other treatments here in Houston, until the tumors go away, or I do. However with the trial and tweaking dosage sizes it looks like my platelets might stabilize, which means I could travel (plane) between here and there so long as I was back to get my treatments. Thus while my trips away from Houston might be short (less than a week) I will be able to leave the city of eternal heat, and see other parts of the world.

On September 25th, Ben went to the ER because he was coughing painfully—he was also having trouble speaking and swallowing. Lisa had just recovered from bronchitis and they thought Ben might be sick too.

SUNDAY, SEPTEMBER 26, 2010

Pneumonia news

-by Lisa-

IT DIDN'T SHOW UP IN the x-ray, but our persistent ER doc ran a CT scan which showed that Ben does have pneumonia in both lungs. Now we've found out that this could instead be a rare side effect from one of the drugs he has been treated with. No way to tell the difference at this point. In either case the treatment is the same: four types of antibiotics through Tuesday. If Ben isn't improving he may need a bronchoscopy.

At least now he's in a private hospital room receiving fluids and pain meds so that his side isn't killing him.

TUESDAY, SEPTEMBER 28, 2010

A busy day for Mr. Morrell

-by Lisa-

IT WAS A WILD TIME IN HOSPITAL room 1221! At least five doctors and a parade of technicians and nurses vied for Ben's attention and body; Ben had two more procedures and we actually got a non-hospital staff visitor. I'll try to make some sense out of it all.

1. Bronchoscopy results: they were just looking for pneumonia, but found that Ben's left bronchial tube is 50% closed up, most likely due to his lymph node and tumor pressing in on it. At the moment this doesn't affect him much, but if it continues to tighten there could be some serious problems. So as a preventative measure, on Thursday he'll be getting a stint put in. This is a sort of internal brace which will keep the tube open. Fortunately, inserting the stint only requires another bronchoscopy (no cutting involved) under general anesthesia (cheer from Ben).

   The only scary part is that there may be

something else in the lung beyond this - the nurses couldn't get a good view of it with Ben coughing. So on Thursday they will also look closer and do a couple biopsies.

2. Cardiograph results: due to the surprises in the bronchosopy, Ben had a cardiograph exam today - like an ultrasound for the heart. He and the tech hit it off and found that the inside of his heart is good and normal. Yay!
3. Barium swallowing test: the theory is that Ben got pneumonia because he is having trouble swallowing. If food is choked on, it can fall into the lungs and cause this kind of infection. So Ben was given a barium-covered mini-marshmallow, which he was miraculously able to swallow in one piece. Its progress was tracked down his throat and showed that it got "stuck" in three places along the way - not swallowed smoothly at all. I guess because Ben's always had a strong gag reflex we haven't taken his swallowing problems very seriously, and neither did the doctors. But now that we know it can hurt him so much it's time to... do something. Yeah, we haven't heard what the plan on this is yet. Probably tomorrow.

This cancer-fighting road has gotten more complicated and discouraging lately.

OCTOBER, HOUSTON

Ben improved greatly and returned home from the hospital on October 5th. On the 14th,he returned to the hospital for a bone marrow biopsy.

THURSDAY, OCTOBER 14, 2010

Thanks

WEDNESDAY I WASN'T FEELING VERY good about the bone marrow biopsy, but I was under the impression they were going to give me a few shots and I wouldn't remember anything. I get in there and she's like, "No we just numb up the area and go in with a big needle!" (Not her exact words, but that was the gist after 5 minutes of talking).

I was slightly surprised at this, semi not too surprised because doctors have lied to me before about what was going to happen in an operating room that, well, didn't. ("Oh no, we'll knock you out and you'll wake up with a shiny new ____________!" In this case it was groshong, but it's more fun to insert "robot leg." Come surgery time: "So when are you going to knock me out?" "What!? We can't do that! You'll be fine, suck it up buttercup, my six year old does these on her Barbies on the weekends, you're cool.")

I finally decided that since I was already there that I would go for it. Two doctors before had said, "Oh, you're so skinny it won't be a problem, there won't be anything to have to dig through to get to the bone." Ok, fine, I can handle small little shots of numbing medication. So they start numbing me up little sting, little burn, little sting, little burn, bump. That felt weird. "Did you hit the bone?"

"We're near the bone, just a bit further."

A sensation, much, much like running your elbow's "funny bone" into a wall, shot up and down my leg combined with a very strange real pain. My eyes must have bulged and I gasped, at which point the person doing the procedure said, "I think perhaps we might have hit a nerve."

They pulled out and my leg had the funny-bone post feeling for a few minutes, they decided to reschedule for another time with the added benefit of drugs. The funny-bone feeling in my leg went away but the added benefit has been pain, like I had been stabbed with a needle, in my upper right hip.

While I am complaining about needles as well the other night when the nurse put in my port it was probably the 3rd most painful time that has gone in. Perhaps needless to say I am very happy to see the end of needles, even for half the day today. (Spent 4 hours at the doctor's to tell me my blood was ok and I didn't need an ultrasound of my liver.)

Sorry if this sounds like complaining, I'm trying to make it somehow funny. Honestly a lot of this stuff ends up being fairly painful on some degree or another, and I try not to complain. It's just sometimes, like Wednesday, everything kind of lines up to be a "bad needle day" or I end up with a mostly funny story about why sitting in a chair hurts right now. So please, take it as funny. Laugh because it's not you, or laugh because you've been there. That's all I ask.

TUESDAY, OCTOBER 19, 2010

How long?

THIS PAST MONTH I REALLY feel like I have been feeling the battle against cancer more than some other months of the past year. When the side effects are hard and heavy and I don't have the mental capacity to think much or to even feel like I COULD be somewhere else, it isn't much more than a day-to-day battle. Yet then there is the type of fight I am in now, where I get treatment once a week and my mind is relatively clear and I am stuck within a week's travels from Houston. And most times I can't fly anywhere. I'm ready for some kind of respite, furlough, or sabbatical from cancer treatments.

Though thinking about it, perhaps what I want is some sort of control over what and/or where I am in the world that isn't dictated by life or death. I guess I've been thinking a lot recently about Seattle and the friends and family I have there, and it's not attainable in my current situation.

I'm sorry if I've been complaining a lot recently. I am tired, more weary, from this constant fight. I have a passion and the skills to do a job that I really love and I would 1000 times prefer to be doing that to this, but here I am.

Is a year really so long? Is the lack of mobility away from Houston really that bad? It's ONLY been a year, how about we look at it like that? And the blessing of Houston is that it's the 3rd or 4th largest city in the US, lacking really nothing I could think to do, and within easy driving distance of a lot of interesting things. God has provided housing for us. God has provided some friends, and while we can't get back to the place we call home we are learning to live where we have been moved.

MONDAY, OCTOBER 25, 2010

Seeing the world

AUBREY, A FRIEND OF MINE, also a cancer patient, posed an interesting question to me the other day, which was essentially: has cancer been worth it? The pain, the suffering, the things I have learned, the people I have met, the places I have (and haven't) gone, etc. When I put them on a scale does it even out? Has cancer been "worth it" to me?

I think perhaps this has been one of the most difficult questions to answer. Do I like pain and suffering and being apart from friends and family? No. On the flip side I have learned SOOO much about generosity, trusting in God, and have met new people in many different places because of this. Odds are very good that if I had never gotten this cancer that I'd be living in Seattle still. And, while I am not super excited about it, here I am in Houston, by way of Colorado Springs. I've got a job I really like (as hard as it can be to do from this afar), we made friends in Colorado, we're making friends in Houston.

Has it been worth it? I would say that I have learned a lot. Both medically and about God (through people). Pain is a pretty good teacher as well. Have I ENJOYED my journey the past couple of years? Sometimes yes, but when it comes to chemo, drugs and cancer, no. Not at all.

But maybe my journey isn't about me (not like there is any ONE why). Maybe I am going through this for you as much as I am for me. I know roughly how many people read what I write, but I don't know who you are, or what you are going through. I just write about what is going on in my life as honestly as possible. Maybe my struggles, pain and suffering serve to encourage you, lift you up, or make you think about something you hadn't thought about before. Maybe God is working through me through this blog the same way He is working through all my friends and family via their generosity.

Anyway, I can't say for sure why I am going through this, but as for worth I think, though it has been incredibly hard, that I have learned some things that are very valuable to me. So yes, this journey has been worth it. Would I choose it for myself or do it again? Probably not.

NOVEMBER and DECEMBER, HOUSTON

THURSDAY, NOVEMBER 11, 2010

I dream in coastal visions

IT'S NOT TOO UNCOMMON FOR me to have dreams about places I have never been to or places that don't exist. Last night I had a dream about a house in a forest on one of the islands in the San Juan Island region. Thinking back on the dream I realized I had brought together different aspects of many different places I would consider peaceful or home-like from the Seattle area.

My life has, obviously, been forever changed because of this disease that is trying to survive in my body. I really don't know from one day to the next, sometimes week to week, what to expect or what is going to happen. A little more than a month ago we decided to make the move down here to Houston until this cancer is dealt with. Not something we had ever planned for our lives. The moves (five in five years of marriage) however haven't really killed the hopes and dreams I had before I got sick, they just got bumped down on the priority list (and new hopes, related to cancer, arose in their place).

Yesterday we were told by the doctor that the cancer was stable to some improvement. So for the time being we'll continue as we are and we'll see what happens.

This time of year though I start to feel the tether more tightly around my neck keeping me in Houston for medical reasons. I feel like we might have won a skirmish in the war, but we're not done yet. I think perhaps as I start to stabilize a bit more that things might get harder. As I have the mind to work, and the desire to travel, it will be harder to be here, especially when I don't feel like anything is wrong.

SUNDAY, DECEMBER 5, 2010

Deserved Frustrations

OVER THE PAST FEW WEEKS I have been continually frustrated by my plans for life. Ranging from the big things like not being able to go to Austin for Thanksgiving to not being able to make it to church some Sundays, or hang out with new friends on some weekday. All of these have been because of my health situation. Cancer, migraines, weakness, coughing, side-effects, etc, etc, etc... the list seems long.

Somewhere in there I got to thinking that some form of being healthy* was something I deserved. Perhaps something I had coming to me because of this past year of horrible health. I don't know where the idea came from, but I hate the word "deserve." I think the connotation is generally only used in a "good" sense: because I worked so hard I deserve a vacation. You rarely hear it used the other way: I broke the law, I deserve a ticket/ fine/ fee/ jail time.

As my health has been in something of a roller-coaster the past few weeks somehow I found myself getting more and more upset, I think mainly at God, for not letting me have some kind of respite from sickness upon sickness, combined with living in a place where we don't have any family, and very few friends. I never said it, but deep down I found myself thinking, "I don't deserve this."

I guess I would like to wrap this up with something deep and life affirming, but I don't really know that it's that easy. This isn't some 30 minute sitcom where you get a problem and an answer in the span of time it takes to cook dinner. I think the solution here is more faith. More trust that God knows what He is doing with my life. Though I can't begin to tell you what that looks like right now. I am frustrated because I can't see/understand what is going on. I need to give that up... go back to the daily fight.

* Relatively healthy that is.

FRIDAY, DECEMBER 31, 2010

Excuse me, I didn't order the Texas...

I FEEL LIKE LISA AND I REALLY hit the ground running at the start of last year. We had had some great visitors at the end of 2009 (my parents and sister) and had some great visits with people in early 2010. We were hopeful and we were tackling the problems before us.

I feel like the mood at the start of this year isn't as bright. We've spent all of 2010 fighting, doing things we really don't like to help the fight, and it seems like the return has been minimal, perhaps even a setback in some areas.

We have learned a lot about ourselves and our friends this past year. We continue to be surprised at what God brings our way to help us through things. In a lot of ways I don't feel like there was a lot of large dark spots in 2010, just a lot of gray. Like the Seattle weather it might not be raining, but the clouds are there to block the light.

Standing at the edge of one year and looking into the next, there are a lot of things I could worry about and fear. There are also things I can hope for. My hope for list is kind of small this year,

I feel like 2010 kind of beat a lot of expectation out of me. I'm not going to worry about this next year, I'm going to try and keep surviving as long as I can and perhaps someday our lives (Lisa and myself) won't be so dictated and defined by one situation.

Here's to another year with more bright spots than overcast days, and perhaps, just maybe, a little rest from the fight.

2011

JANUARY and FEBRUARY, HOUSTON

WEDNESDAY, JANUARY 5, 2011

Buried: Raw

SAYING "I DON'T KNOW WHERE to start" seems like a good place to start. The news we got today from the doctor was not something I would consider good.

Both Lisa and I had been holding out a hope that because I had gotten the full clinical trial this past eight weeks, that the scan would show a little less activity or stability. That wasn't the case. There is a third new tumor spot in my back and the other two spots have shown increased activity, so much so that they took me off the clinical trial.

After our trip to Seattle, we'll be seeing my original oncologist here at MDA about what is next. When last we left him he was talking about a pretty heavy increase in meds.

I'm going to be perfectly honest, I am really, really frustrated by this news. I feel like Lisa and I felt like we were way out front only to turn around and realize we weren't nearly as far as we thought. Like we'd been hiking for what felt like hours and then we pass the 1 mile sign.

I feel pretty purposeless right now. We moved from Seattle to follow a dream and a calling, and now we're in Houston with very few friends and no family. I am having a hard time even knowing what to ask or what to fix. I feel pretty cut free and lost right now. On top of being very, very tired of this battle/war.

Ben started a new kind of chemotherapy at the end of January 2011. It was very hard on his body, and left him feeling confused and drowsy a lot of the time.

MONDAY, FEBRUARY 14, 2011

How I spent my zzzzzzzzzz

THAT IS UNTIL MY ALARM started strumming a Spanish melody this morning at 6:40am (I changed it from the Phantom of the Opera as the wakeup wasn't so gentle). I had my typical blood draw this morning. We were the first folks into the clinic this morning but the waiting room filled up fast. Guess blood is on a lot of people's agendas first thing Monday morning. In a lot of ways this will probably define the week for a lot of people.

The goal of all this blood drawing is to check and see where my platelets are at. On Friday they were at 41, Tuesday previous to that they were at 31. The goal here is to get to 100. When I'm at 100 little bells will go off and alarms will sound and they will re-admit me to the hospital and this whole process will start over again.

Despite the road to recovery the past few weeks I kind of get the feeling like it's time to go back for more chemo again. We haven't knocked this stuff out yet, so the time I spend hanging around really is just more time for cancer to do it's horrible dance of death in my body. It's a catch 22: I want to be able to do things, but I can't really ignore what's inside me and the things that it is going to take, require, for me to remove it.

APRIL, HOUSTON

A March 9th scan showed that Ben's tumors were stable, so his doctor decided to go ahead with more of the same kind of chemotherapy.

TUESDAY, APRIL 5, 2011

Your reminders

MONDAY MORNING AS WE WERE driving to the ER to attempt to clear the semi-mind-numbing pain I was experiencing I found myself wondering if perhaps I was putting more faith in drugs (painkiller) than I was in God. It was something my mind continued to roll over today as I sat on the porch, so I headed to Hebrews 11, the old standby for verses about faith.

I was struck by how much faith is the opposite of relying on things you can see, tangibly put your hands on, and feel for yourself. And then I was thinking about how much of what I am dealing with has to do with what I can feel. I'm not dealing with something theoretical. This is my body, and the pain and the strange feelings are all very tangible.

All of this hasn't led me to the belief I need to give up medicine, grit my teeth, and focus past the pain. I think God has blessed us with some great technology to solve problems. I just realized that Sunday night as I was lying in bed in a bit of pain and thinking about how it would escalate, I never once took the time to pray about it. I didn't take the time to stop and ask God for guidance and wisdom. It was ER now, or ER later.

Ben's doctor informed him in mid-April that some of the assumptions about DSRCT, Ben's kind of cancer, were changing. Another kind of cancer was thought to be very similar to DSRCT, so many of the treatments were copied. However, on closer examination DSRCT turned out to be more unique – and so further study became even more important.

MONDAY, APRIL 18, 2011

What it means

LAST NIGHT I FOUND OUT that Christine and Marvin, friends of ours here in Houston, had a niece die. She had battled cancer for a while and they had done some radical surgery to stem the tide of the cancer. I don't know much but I know she was young, just a kid.

Last night I found myself wondering why I am "deserving" of life more than the thousands of kids that die every day. The answer I came up with is that I am not, in any way, more deserving of anything. God has aided me in this fight against cancer and because of it I've beaten some "long odds" to make it this far, but all of our stories are different and I don't know what is in store for me.

I'm going to be honest, at the start of this year when they kicked me out of the trial, I figured at that point that if I survived through 2011 that it was nothing but the grace of God to get me there (isn't that always the case?). The recent "unknown" by my doctor about this whole thing kind of solidifies that thinking even further. Beyond the next few months it's nothing really other than a black hole.

It's hard at almost any age to be faced with death. I keep thinking of all the fun and exciting things that I am passionate about that I feel like could help the missions org I am part of. Or all the skills God has given me when it comes to computers, writing, etc. I am also faced with wondering why children die with so much of their lives ahead of them. There are so many whys, so many, "what do you want me to do God", and I am confused. I think the abilities God has given me point to one way I should be doing things, and yet the sickness in my body keeps me from doing those things eighty percent of the time. Yet I am aware that God is in control all the time, so this sickness isn't holding Him back from working in/with my life.

I've learned overall that there is no one "why" for anything.

TUESDAY, APRIL 19, 2011

On the Coattails of Dread

PERHAPS A TOUCH MELODRAMATIC. I start chemo tomorrow (or for most of you reading this, today) and I am really not looking forward to it. This whole chemo thing is great as long as you have a goal. Do this chemo until summer, do the trial, kick cancer's butt. Goal. Now it's: do this chemo until... yeah, until then.

I realized that September this year will be the grand two year mark for this bout with cancer. That would explain why I am so tired of drugs, doctors, and different drugs. I have been wrung out and honestly I don't know how I have been able to go for so long without simply burning out (grace of God).

I really, really feel like it would be really nice to be done with this and move onto something else. How about we get rid of cancer and learn things from something else now Lord? How about children? Maybe? Please?

MAY, JUNE, and JULY, HOUSTON

WEDNESDAY, MAY 4, 2011

Overcome?

"**For whatever overcomes a person,** to that he is enslaved."

— 2 Peter 2:19b

I've been wondering lately if I am not somehow being more "overcome" by the situation of my sickness than I should be. I can't help when I am on chemo how horrible I feel, or how sick I get, but I can control the fact that I am getting chemo. We've said before that God has given gifted men and women the intelligence to create chemo and treat the sickness in me, but I find myself wondering if the whole situation has made me something of a chemo "addict"?

People lived and died by the grace of God before chemo, people live and die in third world countries without chemo. People are miraculously healed in places where they don't have chemo. We've been praying for four years that God would heal me. Maybe I need to do something else. These desires and passions I have to be doing something else, to follow the dreams I have, maybe that is what God is calling me to do. Maybe this chemo has reached a point where it has overcome me and I am depending not on God for rescue and redemption, but in chemicals. Maybe they have been obfuscating God's voice in my life.

What if I am being asked to step out in faith that God will take care of me as long as I pursue the dreams and the mission He has set before me. THAT is where I want to be. Not here.

And of course, doubts cling to my mind: "What are you crazy? The thing you are most afraid of in the world will happen if you do that! [Slow death by tumor] You're here in Houston, there are solutions here, experts that 'know' what they are doing. You're safe here. Do you really want to do something like that to Lisa?"

I remember the last time I was faced with something like this... it was a lot less "life and deathy" than this time around. The question was, "Do we move to Colorado and pursue a life there despite my recent 'recovery' from cancer?" We did though. We left the families, the friends, the cities we knew and moved to a place we didn't know to pursue a job that I have always wanted to pursue. It was exciting, it was challenging on many levels, we were learning and we were growing. We were pretty sure that we were where we needed to be. And then I got sick again. Now we've made this move to Houston to try and find a permanent solution to my sickness.

Where do I draw the line? When does the desire in me to be pursuing the things I have been gifted in simply outweigh the weekly unknown of drugs, scans, and doctors? No offense to those that are older in the crowd, but without this cancer I might be looking at another forty to fifty years of life to do what I'm excited about. A lot of the cancer patients I see tend to be at the end of this spectrum. Already at 70 or 80, the fight is part of retirement. That isn't me. I have this fire in me to DO the things God has laid on my heart, this cancer I consider evil because of that hindrance.

Yesterday I was telling a nurse about where the tumors were and I got an image in my mind of a snake with an open mouth behind my heart, his body coiled around my throat/trachea area and his tail dangling down behind my right ribs. This is how I am going to visualize them, and they need to die.

FRIDAY, JUNE 17, 2011

Bought

IN THE PAST 24 TO 36 HOURS or so it has been made known that the bank I currently bank with is being purchased by another bank that has a significantly less than stellar reputation. The response on the Facebook group for the bank has been less than positive, plus there was an article about the change on a blog I typically read and that had a good number of comments as well. The overall gist of the comments has been, "That's it, I'm out."

It has got me to thinking about change that gets forced on us. As my cancer is the two ton elephant on the blog it tends to show up, and in this case it rings true. Cancer has "forced" a lot of change on Lisa and I. From moving, to treatments, to tastes, to looks, to feelings, etc. (the list is long.) The point is if it was up to me I would probably be living back in Seattle without any clue as to other things I could be doing. But, here I am in Houston (by way of Colorado Springs) trying to live a life.

I know things in the consumer realm are different than in the "real life" realm, but the general attitude of "That's it, I'm out!" when the going gets potentially tough, would have been like Lisa running away from me at the first diagnosis. There is a time to bail out of something and run, and then there are times where you need to stay, fight, and maybe make something better because of it.

You never really know what change will bring. I have friends in Colorado, Houston, and frankly all over the world that I wouldn't have had before if not for this. Yes, the fight has been long, hard, crippling, and at times very downhearted, but I feel like I have gained things from not quitting that I wouldn't have had had I run away or quit.

Keep fighting your fights.

TUESDAY, JULY 5, 2011

The Night I Died

"Q: **THERE IS A CURSE THAT STATES** that anyone who possesses the diamond will die!

DW: Well, that's true enough for anything if you wait long enough."

— Dr. Who
exchange with Queen Victoria in episode, *Tooth and Claw*.

This quote, while in a silly context of werewolves and time travel, has struck me at a kind of funny time. The other night I had a dream where I actually died.

I've had dreams where I have been going to die, but nothing where the process actually happened. Fortunately for me this happened in my dream and I was not human at the time. In my dream I was a replicated human life form being used by a government and when I got into contact with others of my kind we all determined that we were too dangerous to be owned by humans and so we killed each other. I went through a dramatic process of shutdown and things just stopped happening and connections to things shut down. I could no longer see but my "brain" was making up images, I could hear for a while then there was a blip of color and I was dead. Which felt a lot like being in a little black box. At which point I panicked and woke myself up.

I woke up a little freaked out, but I was happy to have awoken. It has been weighing on my mind, since the dream, that real life, my life, is different from just shutting something off. God has imbued us with souls that are eternal, and don't just "shut off" when the hardware (our flesh) stops working. And I realized the other night when I woke up that that is a massive hope for me. Cancer, and chemo, it sucks. Not sure how else to say that. This is some tough stuff. I don't know if God has given me 50 more years on this earth or if I won't see the end of the month, but my hope is that when my body shuts down that my soul, who I have given to God, goes on.

It's not a black nothingness of simply, "turning off the machine." There is a whole new life waiting for us. This can lead to a lot of repercussions. If I was living like there was only now and what I experience physically then quite honestly dying would be scary. It's the end of existence. If I am living like there is another existence and part of now is reflected in the "will be" then I really don't have anything to fear from the change. ESPECIALLY since I know that the God who never changes loves me and cares for me.

Life is difficult, there is no reason with God's love that anyone should fear its end. From one adventure to the next!

MONDAY, JULY 18

Friendly, but not really helpful

FIRST OFF I AM GOING TO say that this day went from "tired on the couch" kind of day to "wildly frustrating" in the span of a few hours. I went to a cancer support group tonight (Can Hope) that is held at our church.

I'm going to be upfront about it: probably one of the most frustrating evenings I have had in a very long time. Maybe it's me. Maybe "my generation" finds encouragement in other ways. I don't know. I think being one of the younger ones in the room (there was one other guy there who might have been around my age, but he'd been clear of cancer for over half his life and said he couldn't really remember when he had it) also didn't help. Phrases like, "I was diagnosed when I was 66 and here I am 12 years later!" were kind of grating.

I feel like "success stories" of cancer are a little strange to me, especially when you are telling me to trust God because He's the only one that heals. How about we talk about what you're doing now, or doing differently since you've had cancer. How did it change you? Don't just tell me "I beat it when they said I didn't have a chance!" and then sit down again.

Great, statistically I have a packed cluster of ice crystal's chance in Hades. I am sure you could have filled that room with people who had higher chances of success than I have that didn't make it. Obviously you've survived, how about you tell me what is different about your life now, or what you've learned from it, instead of saying that you lived, and continue to live. WHY!? What is the purpose? There are a HUNDRED things I feel like I have to live for, to do, to see, WHY do you feel it's necessary to tell me you survived? What are you doing with that extra time!?

(And why, oh why God can't I have it?)

THURSDAY, JULY 28, 2011

Doing what the Bible says

LAST NIGHT AS LISA AND I had the privilege of being prayed over by some Elders and other folks at our current church here in Houston (Houston's First Baptist). The last time we were prayed over was before I ever started chemo (back in May 2007). I guess it felt like time to do it again.

Last time it was really a powerful time of being reminded that God was with me through everything I was (and still am) going through. I was surrounded by people I had known a good chunk of my life and who were praying for me to be healed. It was humbling, it was moving, it was a reminder of God's presence.

Last night was different for me in some ways, but at the same time very similar. Last night I was surrounded by strangers, people I really haven't known for more than five or six months (if that long). But at the same time, they were praying to God, asking and imploring Him, on my behalf, for healing and a way out of this.

Believers in Christ coming together to pray about something, sometimes even stuff they have no "vested interest" in, (like my health, or a natural disaster, or even an unnatural disaster) is what continually surprises me about other people. Yes people will reach out and help in physical ways when we barely know them as well, which is so incredibly helpful, but having people praying for me, whom I have never met, and will probably never meet this side of life, continues to blow me away.

I hope for those of you I don't really know, who read this blog, today, tomorrow, or many years from now, that you might get something from this story (as rough as it might be) and know that I have been blessed through prayer.

AUGUST and SEPTEMBER, HOUSTON

A scan in mid-July showed tumors a similar size but with less metabolic activity. The tumors were dying a little. From July 20th to August 17th, Ben was given a little extra time off to recover before his next treatment.

SATURDAY, AUGUST 27, 2011

Mental Update

I HAVEN'T REALLY SHARED WHAT has been going on inside my head lately. That's because, honestly, the stuff inside my head has been a battlefield of yes or no and should I or shouldn't I? And so I have determined to sit down and try to convey the conflict in my head to you.

On one side of the battle we have excitement that this awful chemo is doing something at least. It's not appearing to kill the tumors in a fashion I would like, however it isn't as harsh as it was when I was first taking it. I'm excited by this news and am wondering what that means for me and moving forward.

On the other side I have this sense of "I've been here before." Just as things seem like they are working and the oncologist gives you "good news," after the next PET scan he's going to say something like, "we need to try a different treatment because this one isn't working any longer." And then I'll be devastated because I had hoped for so much.

That is where I am at. I want to hope and be excited for the good news, but at the same time I don't want my hopes to raise to levels that are unreasonable and so when I get "bad news" I end up being depressed for a week.

Of course as I sit and write this (sometimes the best way to communicate with myself {or let God speak to me? To get my own thoughts out of the way so other things can come in?}) I am reminded that my hope isn't in medical skills, technology or medicine. My hope comes from God. That hope doesn't change if I am in the worst pain of my life, or if I am free of cancer and doing whatever it is I love to do.

I guess my trepidation comes in that I am not really sure what God is doing with this cancer and in my life right now. Am I at the end of this trial? Will there ever be an "end of this trial" for me that doesn't end in death? Or is this a fight I am going to take to my grave? One might say I "hope" for a "normal" life, but there isn't anything "normal" about life after cancer. I think I want a life free of hospitals, and* to pursue the dreams that God has given me to pursue.

My hope is in God. Do I know what He is doing in my life? No. All I can really do is hold on and trust that when He says He has the best in mind for me that He does.

I just need to figure out what life looks like living here in Houston with extra free time that includes less foggy chemo time, and perhaps that is some of my fear. What do I do with this time I have been given in a place that isn't where I thought I would ever be?

*I deleted the word "safe" from that sentence... FYI.

FRIDAY, SEPTEMBER 9, 2011

STOP! or not

I MENTIONED IN A POST THE other day that I was mulling over some things. One of the big things I have been thinking about a lot is how my life has stopped and/or continued for the past two, almost three years as I have been on chemo and seeing doctors and moving to be closer to doctors, etc. I say it a lot, but "When this is over I'm going to ___________" (Have fun, fill in the blank!) The thing that I am just now coming to realize (sometimes I'm not the quickest) is that THIS*

IS LIFE.

*(pointing to me and my situation)

When I am better I'm not instantly going to be zapped back to 25 years old and poof, there are your five years back! Look at everything I learned! Now I can get on with my life! Nope: This. Is. It.

In light of that recent finding (feel free to say "DUH!") I am going to try and be a little more purposeful with my time. I feel like I have been drifting the past few years as "healing" was my job. Yes, there were times when I was drastically out of it, and there might be times in the future when I am the same way, but there are too many things I want to do and I can't keep putting them all off "until I get better."

Granted, some of those things might be harder than others at this point (touring Europe in some form or another right now might be kind of difficult) but there are other things. Things like studying something, writing, drawing, re-learning to play the guitar, learning to program, reading more, that could keep me busy here and now, keep my mind engaged, and help me to be a better person when I'm free of this cancer as opposed to "Well, there were some semi-fun video games... and there were some good ceilings I stared at."

Thus, in light of realizing that the "candle" of my life is burning whether I am sick or not, I am going to be more purposeful with the time I have (because frankly at the start of the year I wasn't too sure I'd be this far anyway).

NOVEMBER, HOUSTON

SUNDAY, NOVEMBER 27, 2011

Somnophobia

THIS MORNING I GOT OUT OF BED at six am in an attempt to just WAKE UP and avoid the terrors that had been setting down on me from my post-chemo pull out. I dozed a couple of times today, but largely avoided sleep and am now sitting here writing this entry (and thinking of steak) just shy of midnight. Am I tired? Yes. Did I go to bed over four hours ago because I was so tired? Also yes. Am I trying everything in my power not to fall asleep right now because I am afraid of the chemo dreams? Well, no, but close.

They generally take a few days to ride out and frankly these dreams have always wandered a very strange line. Most dreams, at least in my experience, stay on the side of "Strange enough to not be true" that when I am awake I can figure out the difference between the two. Bull chasing me around a farmhouse in Kansas is scary, but when I am awake and in bed in the middle of Houston I know I don't need to worry about a bull killing me in the next five seconds.

My post chemo dreams are just a step over the line and tend to be violent. They live on the "We'll be right back after you get back from the bathroom" line and only thirty minutes to an hour of being awake and doing something else, can shake the violence, the hauntingness of the dream.

You'll excuse me if I don't go rushing into sleep. It just seems safer on this side for the next few days.

2012

JANUARY, FEBRUARY, and MARCH, HOUSTON

TUESDAY, JANUARY 3, 2012

Milestones

I'M HITTING SOME BIG MILESTONES this year in my life and I wanted to take a moment and share some of those events with you:

First off, this year I am turning thirty. I can somewhat remember when my parents turned thirty. Guess I'm getting "old." Goodbye twenties, I can't say as you have been all that amazing. The first half wasn't horrible, and there were good times, same goes with the second half, but really, perhaps the thirties will be less medical than the twenties.

I feel like, and perhaps I am wrong, there is a

change in the wind when it comes to medical stuff. Either it not being as drastic as it has been in the past, or I can deal with it better, or a difference in drugs... something is going to change. The top of this year though I feel better and more hopeful than I did at the start of last year. Overall I am imagining that I'll need to figure out the intersection of treatments and life a little more than I had in years past.

Speaking of half the twenties, in May of this year I'll have reached the five year mark for having cancer. Back in May 2007 when they told me what I had, they told me I had a seventeen percent chance of living five years. Well, in further proof that numbers mean nothing, and that we don't live by averages, God has blessed me with five years beyond my diagnosis. I'm still fighting, but I've made it beyond the original "good luck getting that far" diagnosis of the first doctor.

On top of all those fantastic things, the love of my life, my tow-truck, buttercup, nursemaid, caretaker, shhh'er, driver, cook, friend, comedian, thinker, architect, and wife, also turns thirty this year. Without her help getting me this far, well, I wouldn't have gotten this far. I know when we said our vows seven years ago this year she didn't expect to be spending five of those years caring for a sick husband, but she has done a remarkable job, and I don't think you'd be reading this now if God hadn't put her in my life.

I share all of this because despite all the moving

and medical issues, God has brought us through it all together. Not just together, but picking up support from friends along the way. I really have no idea what this next year might hold, or how many years I might have left, but all thanks to God for getting me this far!

THURSDAY, FEBRUARY 9, 2012

Excite the Danger

WHAT IS "SAFE"? I HEAR things like, "Dear Lord please keep _______ safe while doing _______." Are we talking safe from harm? Safe from Death? Safe from... a bad sandwich? I've been struck recently by the question of what exactly are we asking for when we ask God for safety.

I don't know that I have ever seen anything in the Bible where serving God would amount to anything I would consider "safe." The heroes of the faith that we read about and admire weren't safe in the least bit. Go ahead, flip open a Bible to anywhere and if it involves a person or people group they most definitely aren't safe.

But isn't that what we love about those stories as well? God brings them through the dangers to deliver them. David, Paul, Isaiah, Daniel, Job, Peter, Jonah, etc. Yes, at some point they ended up dead, sometimes it's recorded, sometimes it's not. Sometimes it was quietly in bed, but for most of them it wasn't.

When we set out to serve God it's not going to be safe. God will help us through tough times, but ultimately the goal is to give HIM glory, and to grow us in faith. There's no way that being safe is going to fulfill that. Tell me, would you rather hear about some harrowing thing that happened to some missionary in Africa, or see vacation pictures from someone's cruise? I mean honestly, which one inspires you more? The danger or the lounging by the pool?*

It's the stories of God's rescuing us that creates a story of redemption that excites us, not a perfectly safe trip there and back. And it's not even for other people. Take me, for example: this cancer (dangerous) has had a million times more effect on me than all the vacations and perfectly safe trips I have ever taken in my life. I'll always remember this. Will I be able to recall the safe trip I had from Seattle to Houston this past month? No, of course not.

God knows this and God uses it. He knows what will bring us and others closer to Him. The downside? It's dangerous. The next time you are faced with praying for someone who is about to head out on a mission trip, or the mission field, or... whatever, and you think about shooting off the old "Keep so and so safe..." line, give it a second and pray something a touch more meaningful, excite the danger in serving God and hope that it'll be a memorable trip where God is glorified, no matter how unsafe it is.

*I am not saying that God can't use a vacation, or that there isn't a time for lounging by the pool. God blesses us with peace and much needed rest. I'm specifically talking about when we send someone out to do something "for God" and asking for safety.

SATURDAY, FEBRUARY 18, 2012

Brave?

PEOPLE HAVE CALLED ME "BRAVE" before for going through what I am going through, though when I think about it, to ME (dictionary.com is going to disagree with what bravery is) bravery is doing something that needs to be done in a selfless fashion. Maybe bravery isn't the word I am looking for. Dictionary.com says, "possessing or exhibiting courage or courageous endurance" which leads to courage: "the quality of mind or spirit that enables a person to face difficulty, danger, pain, etc., without fear."

In my experience there are two kinds of "courage": Selfless, and selfish. Sometimes you hear about people being praised for acts of "selfish courage". They were standing up to X because they themselves wanted Y. Then there are others who will do selfless acts of courage, generally risking life and being in REAL danger, for doing something to possibly help someone or a group of someones.

Much of what I have endured and gone through has been a "Selfish Courage." I fight, I endure, I face difficulty, danger, and pain because I want to live. I don't know if this is really a trait that should be praised or admired. The fact that God has USED that selfishness is evidence of His ability to use anything for His good and benefit of more people than just me. There have been times though when I am really down, or weak, or tired that I do what I do for Lisa, but frankly that is the extent of my "Selflessly facing cancer."

I started this out with a point, and ended up poking myself with the stick of conviction instead. I guess what I am really asking for is that you consider people's motives before you praise them for something. Don't praise me for being motivational, thank God that despite me you have been motivated.

MONDAY, MARCH 19, 2012

My Favorite thing about God

THIS MORNING MARK 2:18-22 landed on my lap and I spent some time looking it over and thinking about it. The part where Jesus says:

"No one sews a piece of unshrunk cloth on an old garment. If he does, the patch tears away from it, the new from the old, and a worse tear is made. And no one puts new wine into old wineskins. If he does, the wine will burst the skins—and the wine is destroyed, and so are the skins. But new wine is for fresh wineskins." (Mark 2:21-22)

This really hit me upside the head, so I decided to dig into it a bit. I went over to Blue Letter Bible, and found a commentary from Chuck Smith where he says:

"The interesting thing about God is His refusal to be patterned. 'Well, God did it this way.' Well, maybe He did the last time, but He wants to do it a different way this time. God does not confine Himself to patterns, and man always makes the mistake when he tries to pattern God, tries to make the groove for God to flow in. And God is always overflowing our banks, and always coming up with some new way of working in the lives of people. And so, God keep us open and flexible and ready to move as the Spirit of God moves in different ways."

As someone who could very easily have been "categorized" as headed for an "early" death years ago when I was diagnosed with a disease that few people survive I really, really appreciate that God is always looking for new ways to get our attention and to bring people closer to Himself. And that He defies patterns. Patterns would have me dead right now.

God doesn't change, but God doesn't always work the same way. That is my favorite thing about God. He wants the best for me, but He's not going to send me down the same path that someone else took to get there.

FRIDAY, MARCH 23, 2012

Shell shocked

YESTERDAY AS THE DOCTORS were piling out of the office (we were their last appointment of the day) one of them turned around and said, "Keep doing what you're doing. It seems to be working. You guys are so humble and positive. Keep it up."

Keep doing what you're doing. I am pretty sure I can attest it's not what I am doing, but what God is doing in me, and what you all are doing for me (praying). When I landed this diagnosis I was pretty sure God didn't want me to slide quietly into the dark, but to fight, and to let other people know what was going on so they would know how to pray and to hope as well.

Yesterday I finally got some news that I had been longing to hear for a long time. Not only are the tumors stable (as they have been going on nine months now) but they have finally started to shrink as well. When we first started seeing this oncologist three years ago he told me it's possible (as the tumors weren't in my bones) that I might be able to live two more years, maybe even kick this thing.

It's been such a long fight to get to this point I guess either it didn't sink in, or I still have the rest of the fight ahead of me and I know I can't slack now. I think I need to take a step back and let it sink in and then spend some time rejoicing in where I am now.

APRIL, MAY, and JUNE, HOUSTON

SATURDAY, APRIL 14, 2012

Dawn again

I KNOW THERE ARE PEOPLE OUT there who are up this early because they are forced to be, and sometimes people I know prefer the night, but really, there are some times where I think you just need to experience a good early morning. I'm not saying it has to happen often, but sometimes just waking up before dawn, getting a bite to eat and enjoying being slower than the world around you and watching it all come awake just makes you feel more than human.

I know I need that... well at least that I am imbued with more than just the strength and ability that this flesh gives me. As I dragged myself to bed last night, head pounding from migraine, just off chemo, and feeling horrible, I thought about where my strength comes from. Frankly it's surprising to me that I have any left at all, which I think only speaks to the blessing that God has given me.

There is a tiredness that resides within me that could consume me whole, and sometimes I wish it would just consume me. But I feel like God has more for me right now and there is much to do still. I just need to figure out what that looks like.

WEDNESDAY, APRIL 18, 2012

How to Hope 101

I LIKE TO GET EXCITED ABOUT things. This might come as a surprise to some of you who know me in various ways and places, but I like the buildup of expectations and then the final delivery of the thing be it an object, experience, or experience.

In the past five years I have really stifled this aspect of my personality. The cancer has been a series of ups and downs; just about the point you start hoping, something catches you in the mouth and pushes down again. And yet on the same side the long hard fights, feeling horrible with no hope of seeing the light and we're given some touch of good news.

Then there are things like planned trips. Lisa

and I really try not to make them because, well, something happens. It seemed our trip to San Diego a few weeks ago was something we kind of snuck up on and were able to go and had a good time. We were hoping to do that again and get in a trip to Colorado, but that got shot down by more medical issues. I allowed myself to get a bit excited about Colorado and it fell through and I was disappointed.

I don't know that I know how to hope anymore. I mean I hope for maybe little things here or there, but long-term (aside from my hope being in Heaven) I really don't know how to do it. Everything else just makes me seem jaded or calloused. Or even mad at God. Which I don't think I am any of those three. I want to hope for things, but in a lot of ways I feel like I've gotten excited about things too many times and it's been taken from me, which hurts a lot. So I'm not sure how to hope for things without getting hurt every time.

WEDNESDAY, MAY 23, 2012

Strangers, Aliens, Friends

CANCER HAS TAKEN US TO some strange places. (Both physically and mentally) Places we never thought we would venture to, visit, or even dare to explore. Because of these travels we have made friends and people have called us friends beyond anything we could have imagined for ourselves. It's not something we realized we needed when we were first set upon this path five years ago, but honestly I can't even begin to fathom what this journey would have looked like without the friends we have had to keep us company, lighten our spirits, and guide us on this rocky path.

At the same time with my chosen vocation I have seen my fair share of people I would like to see more of go somewhere else because that is where their journey was taking them. Like our friends and family in Seattle didn't want to see us go, we were following something we wanted to do, and something that we felt God was opening up before us. Then as we were in Colorado Springs we made friends, and then watched them go other places in the world. Then it was time for us to pursue the death of my tumors so we too left. Leaving behind people who continue to pray and support us and look forward to our return. We were welcomed to Houston by people we didn't know. We were strangers, aliens to this world and culture, but they soon became friends.

Now, as God has given me this much life I seek to make it easier for people to go from being strangers in a place to friends. This is kind of two sided.

On one side I really want to get to know people. To really dive in and make a connection. At the same time I am afraid of getting too close because they might leave to go somewhere else, or (as is a very real possibility with helping people with the cancer I have) they might not be around in a few years.

In Colorado Springs I felt like we were at a hub of activity. People always coming in and going out and moving around. It was hard not to be a little bit envious of those people who would drop in with stories of far off places and countries and what God was doing there, and then they'd be off again.

I guess what I am saying is that I think this is a sign that you are growing in Christ and a maturing Christian. Are things changing? Do you have people in your life who are helping you grow and then moving on and encouraging you to help other people grow? We aren't plants. We don't grow on our own and then fade and die alone. At least that's not how it's supposed to work.

Not really where I wanted to go when I started this blog entry... but here we are. Life lessons from Ben.

FRIDAY, JUNE 8, 2012

Glorified

On Wednesday when I eventually saw my doctor he came in and explained that the tumors were still shrinking despite being off chemo for nine weeks. He proceeded to explain to us and his fellow what he had done with the protein study of the tumors of the DSRCT patients he had.

At the end of the time he reiterated that he was really quite, what was it? "Pleasantly surprised" by the progress my tumors had been making. This is a guy who spends all day dealing with cancer patients and is considered an expert in his field for my type of cancer. They had set up an appointment to start more chemo the next day already, so the feeling I was getting was that the expectation was that the tumors would have stopped shrinking and would have started to grow. He was expecting this and he was prepared for the next step.

INSTEAD, God has worked in my body and continues to shrink those tumors. Be it through the medical treatments I have gotten for the past year and a half, or through methods of His own, He has brought me safe thus far, and now I am getting three months off.

I was explaining to my small group last night that I feel like a dog who has just been let off his chain for the first time in a few years. Can I run and go explore other places? Is that ok?

I am happy about the news... but at the same time I want to convey to you that THIS reaction needs to be the same no matter if I get three months off now, three months off later, or it comes storming back with a force. God's will for my life is the important thing. If he wants me to be well enough to do what I feel like He has called me to do with my health (whatever level that is at) then I need to do it. Three months off doesn't change anything.

These tumors are still like bombs in my body, at this point I just get a bit of a "summer break" to make it happen. It's exciting, but we also don't want to lose sight of the greatness of God in this.

THURSDAY, JUNE 14, 2012

The heat of Summer

SEASONS... EVERYTHING AND EVERYONE goes through them. At the moment I'd say I am just about to enter the summer of the past three years of chemo and cancer treatments. Winter was a year and a half to two years ago, and the spring time has been this past year as my body has gotten used to the side effects of the chemo and it has been actually working.

I have no idea how long summer will last, but like all things it will be a season. Summer will bring with it its own challenges that Winter, Spring, and Fall don't have. There are some ways in which the other seasons are easier than this one. That is also because each season involves change. There is a time in each of the seasons where I pause and say, "It's now a new season." I might not see it coming, I might not see it going, but I can tell when I'm there.

Lisa and I have been transplanted here to Houston and we have spent literal seasons here, and we are approaching a new season here spiritually as well. This is something I've been thinking about. Is Houston our "hard seasons" city? We are looking forward to spending a summer in Colorado Springs and Seattle, and at the same time I am wondering if we aren't "shipping off our fruit" as it were. I think we did this in Seattle after my first seasons of cancer. We jetted to Colorado Springs as soon as summer arrived... and it looks like we're doing something like that again.

Am I, are we, cutting out a vital part of our relationships with people by cutting out too soon? I assume God knows best where to "deliver" the fruit that has been growing in us these past few seasons. I just wonder sometimes if my will to "survive" and "be alive" might be a louder, stronger voice than what God, the farmer, wants to do with me, the tree.

Please Lord, help me to not forget in the heat of Summer what I fought so hard for in the dead of Winter and the growth I have gained along the way. Help me to be nourishment to others no matter where we end up, and shade for the weary who are in different seasons than I am in right now. Use this tree Lord.

WEDNESDAY, JUNE 20, 2012

See what He Brews!

HEBREWS 11 THOUGHTS: This is the famous "By Faith" chapter that talks about the heroes of the faith. It's pretty cool to go through and think about the people he both implicitly names and then only hints at. I am afraid with the common popularity of teachers and pastors of shaming fellow US citizens for how blessed we are and not doing anything about it that the real power of this chapter might get lost in shaming people.

The real power of this chapter lies not in shaming us for what we have, but to inspire us to action. Look at all these people, who armed only with faith literally did the impossible and did things for God that no one else has done before, nor has done since. This chapter should make you get up out of your chair and raise your fist into the air and say, "Yes! I can do anything through Christ who strengthens me!" and know that no dream is too big for the kingdom of God. Faith is our power to do the things that God wants to do on this Earth through us.

It's not for US that God wants to do these things, but for Himself, and drawing others to Himself. How amazing would it be at the end of your life to look back and see everything that God had used you to do? To not only be another tool in the tool shed that had helped make many houses, but to be a well used tool. Not something left in the box, but something that has duct-tape holding it together, maybe a few other parts holding it together, and very, very obvious that it was a favorite tool of the designer.

That's what I want. I might not be listed in a

list like this of the ancient heroes of the faith, but I hope at the end of my life I can look back and see where God has chosen to use me, and where I let myself be used. It seems safer to be a tool that never gets used. You'll never get chipped, or worn, or broken. But to be used is exciting, dangerous, and you are serving your purpose.

(Ironically from a faith perspective the places of "safety" and "danger" are reversed from what you might normally think.)

This is my hope for all of you reading this. That you will let God use you, and that you will be a tool for the Lord powered by some crazy amounts of faith that defies all logic.

JULY, AUGUST, and SEPTEMBER, HOUSTON

SATURDAY, JULY 28, 2012

Greatly, Deeply

"Whom God will use greatly, He will wound deeply."

— A.W. Tozer

Several things come to mind by that quote that I couldn't stay asleep for, so I thought I would blog.

First, despite the order of the words, it's generally thought God will bring something into your life that will hurt to a great extent in order to be able to use you. It's part of a preparation. And sometimes it doesn't happen quickly... sometimes it takes a long time. Though the great thing is that we can have confidence that God is, and/or will be using us! And honestly, what's better than being used by the maker and creator of the universe?

Second, the quote says nothing about healing. I am reaching a really strange place (it seems to me) where I am becoming OK with having cancer (it's not a fight I'll stop, mind you). I prayed and asked fervently for healing in the past five years, and honestly I wonder if I should have been praying for complete trust in God instead.

It's like getting put on a roller coaster. You will get jerked around, go up, go down, maybe even do a barrel roll, but when you're praying for it to be over, it's not like the ride is just going to stop and let you off. There is a course. You have to have faith that the designer of the ride went to school, got an engineering degree, did all the right math, etc etc and that the ride, despite being scary as all-get-out is going to bring you to the end in one piece (this analogy isn't perfect, don't take it too far...)

The point here is that I'm on a course that God has set me on. Do I like it? Would I choose it again? Would I give it to anyone else? Does it matter what I think? I told God many times, in many places, "Send me. I'll do what you want me to do. I'll obey you." This is God saying, "Ok. Here's a lesson in trust."

I can't say life will be easy, and honestly if I

want there to be some meaning to my suffering, or some purpose to life after death, then I have to believe that God wants the best for me. Getting my attention off of myself and my mundane life to thrust me into something greater takes a lot more than some "still small voice" that I can ignore for the booming of my Xbox.

MONDAY, AUGUST 13, 2012

Wrestling and Imploring

I WOKE UP ABOUT THIRTY MINUTES ago (It's 3:50am MST) and there is a great pain in my body. Since Friday I think it's been getting worse and frankly it's been weighing on my mind a little more than normal. I used to take my cough/pain medication to deal mainly with the cough and then up it around chemo time to keep the pain at bay... the past few days I have been taking it less for the cough and more for the pain.

I've spent the last thirty minutes or so praying and doing what some might consider "wrestling with God"... but that would imply I had any strength with which to do that. I am reminded of Jacob in Genesis 32:22. Several things stick out to me in this: Jacob didn't go down without a long fight (all night!), and in the end God (again) blessed Jacob. There was tenacity there in Jacob's spirit; he wouldn't let go, and God honored that.

I was thinking that with my lack of strength

though that what I am doing is more like one of the many petitioners to Jesus when he was healing the sick. In many ways I feel more like the leper in Mark 1:45, "imploring" God to heal me. I don't know what that leper had to go through, but from everything I have read on lepers in that time period it wasn't easy. There was a fight, he sought God and asked that He would change the course his life was heading.

A question came to mind this morning as I was praying and frankly it's been really hard to deal with, and I want to share it with you. I've said before that there is never any one "why" to this kind of situation I'm in. To think there is only one answer for why I have been given cancer is kind of shallow, and lacking in an understanding of how God uses people. This leads up to the question that I feel like God brought to mind this morning: "If continuing to be sick meant that more people could come to understand more deeply and personally about God, would you really be so selfish as to want to be healed?"

I know the "right" answer to that question. But saying yes and asking God to use me HOWEVER He wills, is a lot closer to my open wound than simply asking God to heal it and for me to "move on."

Do I have a rare disease that few people will ever hear about, much less get? Yes. Do I want to use that opportunity to tell people what God has done for me? Yes. But where am I drawing the line? "Ok God, five years of cancer. It's been a great run, I've got some great stories, and you've really inspired some people through me. We're finished with this and can move onto something else now right?" It's the "I'll go this far and no more" mentality.

Some of my co-workers whom I look up to have served God in other countries, and in difficult situations, for the past 20 or more years. How is this any different?

After having the summer off to heal from cancer treatments because his tumors were stable, Ben was mentally preparing to get a scan to see what had happened with his tumors over the summer.

FRIDAY, AUGUST 31, 2012

Steeled

WHEN VISITING THE ONCOLOGIST IT'S never been all that great of an idea to go in optimistic. Odds are good that you will be disappointed. It's better to go in and assume you're going to hear "There is nothing more we can do" and instead hear, "Well, the tumors are stable, but they aren't shrinking at all" or "The tumors have grown a bit..." Emotionally it's a lot easier to come up, than be up and come down.

I like to be optimistic, but in these cases you have to know also how to protect yourself and not to get hurt. It also means that if you're right, and they DO lay on some bad news, then you nod knowingly.

I have to confess with the way I have felt the last three weeks that I am not expecting good news. And honestly that scares me a little bit. I am tired, I am in pain, I feel sick. These are signs. I don't know what else to say. It's not going to be an easy weekend.

SUNDAY, SEPTEMBER 2, 2012

(Un)informed Faith

Where is the line between information and faith? I think it comes down to this: Have I pursued God first? All the Googling on the planet won't get me the answer that God wants me to be holy... and ultimately that is what God wants from us.

Realistically do I know what is going to happen on Wednesday with the results from my scan? Factually, no, I don't know. Spiritually, I do know. I have confidence that no matter WHAT those scans might show the doctor that the outcome will be the same, God will be making me more holy. There is where I can put my faith, and there is where you can put yours as well.

TUESDAY, SEPTEMBER 4, 2012

Why Holiness?

HOLINESS IS EMULATING GOD. Why do I want to emulate God? The Bible is full of perfectly good examples and reasons. A very deep part of me wants to emulate God, to try and be holy, because selfishly I hope it'll get me out of this problem (cancer). I'm aware of it. It's not easy, and I don't want to make you think I have somehow been perfected in my sickness.

No, I want to live, I want to see what God will do with me... but frankly a LOT of the reasoning behind that is selfishness. God's called me out to be different (wow! Awesome!). And now I want to stick around long enough to see what that looks like for other people. I know God uses everything, and He has been using my selfish desire to stay alive in your lives.

I want you to know that holiness is something I am striving for. I say I want what God wants, but what if what God wants is my death? What if God wants me to live in horrible horrible pain and suffering? What then? Do I still want what God wants? How far will I follow? Where is the line?

Last night as I was word studying holiness I came across a comment that suggested the dichotomy of the Greek for holiness (hagios) was hagos, which translates "an awful thing." Sanctification... holiness, being more like God, isn't easy, and though it might be something we say we want, don't we really all view the process as "an awful thing"? Isn't that why I am asking you all to pray for me to be healed? Isn't that selfish? How far am I really from wanting what God wants? Do I choose, will I continue to choose, the awful thing if it brings me closer to God?

NOVEMBER and DECEMBER, HOUSTON

WEDNESDAY, NOVEMBER 28, 2012

Everything comes to an end

I'M NOT GOING TO SUGAR coat anything for you all. The doctor is reaching the bottom of his "bag of tricks." He's not going to put me on high dose Ifosfamide unless it's a last ditch effort because he doesn't think I can take more than 2 or 3 doses before it becomes unsafe for him to give me more. He's going to put me in contact with the doctor I had before who did the drug trials.

He told me flat out that if nothing works I can expect maybe more than six months to survive. He says three months would go fairly smoothly, and then things would start getting more rough.

All my tumors have grown in my body. So nothing like what I had hoped for, but my hope is in the Lord, not in the things that my doctor can think up.

Though I have to admit I am more than a little disappointed by the news. When I first visited the doctor he told me that I could probably expect to live two years. Here we are at three and a half years. It's becoming very obvious that there aren't many other options here. I am not going to start grasping at ANYTHING to try and get results (hold back your email forwards please...) but I might start looking around if MDA doesn't have anything that can do anything to these tumors.

I am sorry this is so fragmented and partial, but I am not in a very eloquent mood right now, and felt I needed to get the facts out.

SATURDAY, DECEMBER 1, 2012

Friday night Prayers

LAST NIGHT **NATE AND BROOKE,** some friends from our church, called a prayer session for Lisa and I. People showed up, I think the enemy also tried to influence it, but most importantly our God was there mightily.

Probably upwards of thirty people showed up. I say that I think the enemy also tried to get in as well/set back what we were doing because almost as soon as we started I got one of my migraines where I lost all of my sight. The migraine progressed somewhat like normal but it took a back seat to what was going on in the room.

I have never experienced a more heart-felt time of prayer in my life. People were crying, imploring the Lord, reading scripture, sharing stories of healing and the Holy Spirit's guidance of doctors. I was prayed for very deeply, as was Lisa.

It touches me to think that my friends, even some people I don't know that well, would show up and cry out to God to bring me complete healing.

I have a confession to make. Wednesday, I lost hope. In the past when they have said, "You have X amount of time" I have just kind of shrugged it off and said, "I have what time God has given me." Wednesday it went right into my heart and I believed it. I had laid down my sword and was pretty much taking the arrows that were being fired at me. Hope was something that was being strangled beside me as I let myself take the lies and the belief I had this was the end.

This morning is the first time... in I don't know... ever? That I have woken up with praise songs running through my mind. I almost physically felt like I held a sword in my hand. It brings me to tears with shame to think of the things I had believed and given up on my God. Forgive me Lord, my father, for sinking in the pit of despair and thinking that this fight was over and ended before you said it was.

I cry too for the faith that my friends had when I did not. To build a chain together and reach down into that pit and pull me out back into the light. To continue that fight for God, to continue the fight toward HEALING, for God's glory.

This morning I don't know if I am feeling physically stronger... I can't really tell over the overwhelming new spiritual outlook I have this morning. Thanks to my God were first upon my thoughts this morning and I cannot tell you what a difference that is compared to the "You're going to be dead in six months" that has greeted me the past few mornings.

SUNDAY, DECEMBER 9, 2012

Climbing up hills

I WAS THINKING ABOUT IT THIS morning and I realized that I really want to be healed (despite knowing that Heaven is on the other side) because I feel like there is so much more work to be done. He's given me a passion for things that need doing in certain areas, and I would really like to have the strength and energy to do them. BUT (like the boys in the fiery furnace) if God chooses not to rescue me from this I would hope that I could inspire more of YOU (that I both know and don't know) to do those things, or fund those things, that I have a passion for.

Sometimes God tells us no. I understand that.

And really the other side of "no" is Heaven for me. I have a thousand thousand things that I would like to do and get done here, but God, ultimately, knows what is best for me, all of you, and how my sickness plays into that. I want to let you know that if God chooses to go a route none of us wanted or anticipated, that that is, more than ever, His plan, which is good and right and better for all of us.

THURSDAY, DECEMBER 13, 2012

Pills, Costs, and Worth

LAST NIGHT AS I WAS TAKING pills I realized that I put down 170 dollars' worth of pills, and next week when I go to taking twice the amount I will be taking about 350 dollars of pills a night. Needless to say I would MUCH rather be putting that money into a fancy dinner or vacation than 6 little pills. Oh well... at this point what's another 10k when I've crested 750k so far in the attempt to prolong my life.

It has always made me wonder if the money being poured into my treatments is/has been worth it. While I know you can't really and honestly put a price on human life I have always wondered if those funds might have gone towards something that would have saved more lives. But then I think about it and realize that there is no way some insurance agency would have used that money in some other fashion. It would most likely have lined someone's pocket instead of going to some greater good.

It's kind of one of those "hypothetical questions" that never really could be answered. If the insurance company (in an attempt to save money) had come to me and said, "Here's 300,000 dollars to not take treatment" if I would have taken it. I'm not sure if I would have then (most assuredly not) and I probably wouldn't take it knowing what I know now (well, if they offered me that kind of deal NOW I might take it, but not back then...) A lot could be done with that kind of money.

The point of this little exercise is really just to showcase what goes on in my head sometimes, asking if the cost has been worth it. At this point in my life I can say yes... All the pain and the suffering has been worth it. If nothing else I have learned a lot about myself, my friends, my family, and my God.

Has it been difficult? Yes. Would I do it again? Errrr, I think I would probably still land on the "no" category still. Though, that is what makes God in control of my life and not me. I would not choose the kind of life I have had, in the past five years, for myself. But it has been far better for me than I could have planned.

WEDNESDAY, DECEMBER 19, 2012

Process with Thanks

THE PAST FIVE DAYS HAVE been unexpected, more painful, and more frustrating than any other time that comes to mind this past year. We KNOW we should try and keep an open hand when planning. Both so if God wants us to do something with us and/or I get really sick. (Which is also God asking us to do stuff.) This time around though we thought we had a green light, so we were proceeding, when we got what we thought was a yellow light. It was in fact very red and we had to retool what we thought we knew and were allowed to do. Sometimes I think I can see some of why God does something, but a good chunk of the time I am just flat out confused.

I really don't know why God has had me in the hospital for the past five days, but I've learned the best way to deal with the frustration and confusion is to thank Him. Dear Lord, thank you for my voice, my readers, everyone who prays for me, the medical staff, and on and on. It's very easy when I'm frustrated or confused when I felt like God told me to do something and now I'm stuck somewhere else.

"Thanks" starts to provide you and I with perspective. You know what? I might not be able to make it to Colorado Springs for two weeks like I wanted, but I am thankful we have family to see at Christmas time, a car/resources to get to Colorado, family that loves me, friends who will bend over backwards to help, and the list goes on. That really is the beauty of giving and living my life to/for God. He loves me and is going to do what is the best for me. He loves me equally to how he loves my wife, my parents, my siblings, etc. He knows; nothing is going to be a mistake, it might be a delay in the adventure you and I had planned, but I cannot think of a time when God took me somewhere and I wasn't amazed or impressed by something God taught me, a person I have come into contact with, or I was able to be there for someone when they needed me when normally I might not have been. The list of things goes on and on.

I've heard these called "Divine appointments", but in reality it's just a life God is using. You only see doctors on special occasions, so that is why I think "Divine appointments" doesn't accurately cover the fact that if you are open to it, this will be your life. Confusing and frustrating if you don't remember perspective. Again, where "thanks" comes in. I thank God for everything He's given to me in this situation, and the thing I was frustrated about fades away as I learn to accept the thing that God has for me right here and now.

MONDAY, DECEMBER 24, 2012

A Fear - Realized

I **HAVE ALWAYS THOUGHT THAT** if I got better (as in healed from this horrible cancer stuff I am going through) that it would be amazing to reach out, to be around, to be available for others that have this same thing. Earlier this year I started to do that. I joined the DSRCT support group and found a couple guys who came to MDA and met up with them and tried to connect with them on issues of life.

One of the things I thought of back when I was in early stages of diagnosis when I had this idea was that it would be a heartbreaking work as most DSRCT'ers don't live beyond the 2.5 year mark. The past few months, one of the guys I had met with, talked with, and gotten to know better, swapping stories of life, hospitals, and God (I even linked to his blog here once) died this morning. While I am incredibly thankful that God finally took him away from the incredible pain he was in, it just makes me remember that there are people left behind with this sickness. He had a wife and several kids.

My "fear" was that I would find other people who are suffering/have suffered what I am going through and that I would only get to know them for a short time. Ultimately a reflection of life on Earth, we meet and the time we have together is but a breath. But, no matter what happens to my health, I feel like this is really something that God has called me to do. I hope I never get jaded, no matter if I do this for the next few months, or if I do this for the next thirty years.

A side note: I've heard some people say that they had family who just "knew" when it was time to go. While every day brings my hope and desire for Heaven that much closer, I also continue to find new things I want to do here. Ways to help others, things to write, things to say, things to learn, things to convey to others... I don't feel like it's my time, the fire of passion and desire to help still burns brightly.

MONDAY, DECEMBER 31, 2012

Farewell 2012

AT THE START OF LAST YEAR I looked at 2012 ahead of me with what the doctors were saying and told God, "If there is any way I am going to get through 2012, it'll be only by your grace and mercy."

Here I am now, sitting at the cusp of 2013, and God brought me through 2012. I am here now to say that God brought me safe through 2012 when I had doubts to whether I would live through it or not.

NOW as I look at 2013 ahead of me they are saying things like they don't expect me to make it beyond April. That combined with the loss of another DSRCT friend of mine this past week really rings loudly in my head. I have accepted that I am mostly ready for death, the pain and the agony of this cancer would be great to be over... but at the same time a few things this past week have really awakened me to the desire to live as well.

The first one was talking to Ray, my boss, this past Friday about stepping down and the future of missions (I am part of a small group of people at OC that are trying to take a look at what the future of missions looks like. Mostly we are running off of a model that was put in place 60 years ago that has seen little change since then. With the world being far more connected and people wanting to help, without being "full time" missionaries, we need to change, or we need to move aside for the next generation. But ultimately we hope to bring in the new generation and to connect Christians all over the world in spreading the Gospel. Meaning locally and internationally. But those lines are so blurred these days the only real difference in some of these things is distance... and even that can be bridged fairly quickly). At the end of the discussion I was super-energized and full of ideas. I was ready to quit doing IT and become head volunteer wrangler right there and then.

The thing this taught me was that there are still a LOT of things I would like to do and/or try, not just in the IT arena, but in getting people involved in missions in some way or another.

The second thing that kind of gave me a new hope for life was in saying goodbye to my brother. I really enjoy spending time with him and doing stuff with him. The times we have spent some time together, doing a project, planning a meal, or just doing something, has really energized me. Creative interactions with my sister are the same for me as well. I feel like each of us Morrell children bring a different aspect of creativity to the table and when we get together to do something it turns out to be amazing. I feel like I have only scratched the surface of what Morrell sibling collaboration might look like. I'd love to have more years to see about doing more things with them.

2013

JANUARY, HOUSTON

TUESDAY, JANUARY 1, 2013

Perhaps

I THINK PERHAPS I AM AFRAID to go to sleep because when I wake up it all might be different. But as the hours crawl onward, further into the new year, nothing has changed. The city, the people all sleep, to wake tomorrow and go on about their lives. Another year, another six months, another week... does anything really change that much?

It came as a screeching halt to my life in May of 2007, what will be six years ago, when they said I had cancer. It all changed. The way I tell time, the way I feel time going by. Sometimes in drops, and other times in torrents that, no matter how much I grasp at it, it can't, or won't, come back.

Almost six years past my sentence of death... more time than some have been given, and at the same time less than others... but who can really claim to know when that last breath will come? Even at 90 there will be someone who has lived longer, taken more breaths, lived through more, than me.

Time continues on... days roll up in weeks and weeks become months and months, years... I feel them differently than before that day in May. Yet, they act the same as they did every day up until that point. I am aware of my minutes and I feel like I can't plan for any kind of future. Being able to tell what is happening a week from now seems like a huge blessing. I can't even imagine writing an event on my calendar for next year with any kind of confidence. Yet, most of you do.

Would I change if tomorrow I was healed? Would I revert to the way I was before? Is that what really keeps me from being healed? That God knows I would go back to pre-2007 me if given the chance? Or would I? Would I live differently with the burden lifted? Or would I be replacing one burden for another?

What is the cost of healing? Knowing that I am prepared to die and then, being somewhat confident of the when, the how, it is replaced with a giant question mark that hangs over everyone else (that is generally just ignored). What else? Could I ever stop talking about how God had saved me? Did the three friends of Daniel (Daniel

3) ever stop telling people about what God did for them at the fiery furnace? How could I be silent? Would the desire to tell the world burn me out? How could I tell everyone? How is being saved eternally through Jesus Christ any different? Why don't I tell more people about that? That's more important than being free of cancer... yet here I am not saying much.

Sometimes it seems like God uses dead people more than he uses the living. In the face of death we leave statements, comments, memories, and then, we die. And in that death, shock-waves of effect on the friends and family we touched momentarily before our deaths... Is my story worth more with the final punctuation point on the end? Or does it matter? We don't really know if the apostle Paul was killed or not. Some traditions have him going to Spain and retiring there. His story begins and ends with a few letters in the New Testament.

At this point I don't know which way I'd go. I think there would be some remarkable story for everyone to tell about the sickness being removed from me and the effects that story could have. But then how I face death, how I face the end, might be just as powerful a story. Or maybe the end doesn't matter. Maybe it's the fight that is the point of this story. Maybe whether I live or die isn't the point. We all want a happy ending to our stories, and barring that some kind of closure, but what if the point of MY story wasn't about how it ended, but how the whole thing was fought?

I don't know what God will choose to do with my story, my life, but I pray it has been, and will continue to be effective. I also hope the "ending" (be it life or sickness) is also as meaningful. I'm not really sure which one will end THIS chapter but I am looking forward to it as much as the rest of you.

Thank you Lord for bringing me this far. Give me wisdom on how best to tell the story you have given me, and how to share the saving you have already blessed me with.

FRIDAY, JANUARY 4, 2013

Increasing/Decreasing

THIS WEEKEND LISA AND I are trying something new. I don't want to give any details of it until we've done it, but we'd really like some extra prayer on Saturday and Sunday.

I was really sick yesterday. I woke up feeling like I had a rock in my stomach and once I had tried to expel it I just felt horrible all day. I barely ate anything and then at dinner time I had some food and felt pretty sick again. Went to bed again and felt kind of the same this morning, but I got up and did some things and the feeling eventually faded (as in around 1pm).

I think the chemo is accumulating. Who knows if it'll do anything other than turn my hair white and make me feel horrible... you know, in this whole process the "getting better" part has been the part that has hurt the most. I think that is the opposite of the way God heals. When Jesus heals in the New Testament people don't scream in pain for hours on end and then get up, shakily, and say, "I'm healed!" No. Jesus, or one of His disciples says, "Be healed..." and they are. From top to bottom. Healed. Better. No more sickness. Pain. Whatever troubled them before, is no longer troubling them again.

In my previous post I wondered about if my story went beyond the sickness. What about all those people in the Bible? We hear about them getting healed, sometimes leading up to their sicknesses (He was crippled from birth, etc.) but once God heals them we really don't hear about them again or anymore. The one leper did go away and come back to say thanks, but I guess the narrative of the Bible is about Jesus, not about what happened to sick people who were healed.

Ultimately I think this is what made me wonder if I was healed what I was supposed to do with it. I think John's description and the example of the New Testament are pretty good examples. "He must increase and I must decrease." (John 3:30) Either way, I die and live no longer, or I am healed and live X more years. The story is about how I come to know more about God and trusting in Him and what He is doing. In the end, HE must increase, and I must decrease. It's no longer about what Ben can do for God in the world, it's what

God is doing in the world, and how YOU can help. I'm in the background, helping where I can. Ben is decreasing and God is increasing. If the best way for that to happen is the end of my life, then well, that answers that question. If God wills it then there are still things on this earth that I can do to help HIM increase in other people's lives, while decreasing my own.

This is of course counterintuitive to the way the business works. What do you want to do in business? Get ahead, make more money, be the guy at the top calling the shots. I think from a Christian perspective being given a position of leadership in a for-profit company would be really difficult (also not where I am gifted... so to each their own... and I won't say it's "bad" or anything to be an executive. God has gifted us each in many different ways and the story He has for you isn't the story He has for me). John died so that Jesus could increase. I can't say as I am any better than John, or any biblical character, but this is my story. I can see a lot of ways that are exciting about what God could do in the future, and would LOVE to help be a part of that. But it's not about me. Which, really, is what makes this whole thing so exciting.

I have a fight to fight right now, but it is my hope, my prayer, that after I have learned the things that God wants me to learn from this, that He would heal me and allow me to pursue HIS increase all the more.

WEDNESDAY, JANUARY 9, 2013

Dodging Potholes

I DON'T KNOW HOW TO RESPOND any longer to people who ask me to pray for things that will go smoothly, safely, or that some event that looks like it could be a huge thing would be nothing. I am pretty sure God uses each and every bump, ding, scratch, fender-bender, or totality to teach us more about Him. When we ask God to "Please keep so and so safe..." or "Quickly heal whatshisname..." aren't we essentially asking God to make our lives easier at the price of getting to know Him better?

I am not saying that there isn't a time and a place to ask God for things like healing, or safety, or... stuff. But isn't it always the first thing we ask for? The past couple times we have driven back and forth to Colorado I have had a really hard time with this. There is so much road, so many possible connections we could make with people between here and there, I felt like asking God to give us a safe trip might mean that we miss something, or someone that God would have liked us to experience or encounter (though, full disclosure, He has given us safe trips).

God answers prayers. Are we asking for things that are dulling our lives? Think about it: we don't tell stories of safe travel or regular afternoons. "So THEN after making a perfectly safe drive from Houston to Amarillo we drove AROUND the city and safely made it to Colorado Springs without incident." Not only is that a boring story by anyone's reckoning, but it's forgettable, and no one learned anything. It's the harrowing stories, the close scrapes, the scares that teach us something about ourselves, our friends, our family, and our God. It's those stories that we tell to our children, our grandchildren, and those stories that we remember when we talk about God's goodness to us.

I want to make it clear that God does invite us to ask Him for things, but in the asking perhaps we should be open to realizing that God wants us to know Him better, and while studying the Bible is a great tool for that, it is only head knowledge, and not experience. That is where we learn about faith, that is where we grow our faith is in the meeting of head knowledge and our experiences of God.

What a Trip!

EARLIER I MENTIONED THAT I WAS going off the grid and Lisa and I went away for a few days. The only thing I mentioned was that we were going to "try something new." Now it's time to share the details.

A month or so ago a friend of mine who used

to live in Seattle sent me a Facebook message and said, "Hey, we have a friend here in New Orleans whom God has been using to heal people around the city. Maybe you guys should come see him and we can also hang out and have some fun."

Having never been to New Orleans and never had ANY connection with faith healers I have to admit I wanted to see New Orleans, but I also didn't want to get my hopes up. I trust God to do healing, we see it in the Bible as Jesus walks among the people. The church I came from in Seattle holds to the idea that healing was a gift that had been used to spread the gospel at the start of Christianity, and then was something God doesn't use anymore. I frankly don't know where that idea came from... I don't know why God would be different today than He was before. He's the same God yesterday, today and tomorrow. He healed then, He gave people the ability to heal others, why not continue that today? The gospel still needs spreading. These were things I was wrestling over the few weeks after the prayer session they had for me here in Houston.

We got back from Colorado and I contacted my friend and said, yeah, let's make this happen. So we drove out to New Orleans and not too long after we arrived we met with the guy who our friend had said that God was using. We talked for a bit and then he prayed for me for a while. Putting his hands on different places of my body as he prayed. He particularly focused on my right side about half-way down.

I wasn't sure what to say after the meeting with him because frankly I didn't know if I felt any different. (It would probably be hard to say because of how "sneaky" this cancer is about not being felt until it's way too late.) However that night I didn't take my extra strength long-lasting pain killer to see what would happen the next day. Since Saturday I have cut my pain meds from 36mg to 12mg (sometimes less).

I was also holding off saying anything about it because I had a scan yesterday and I was curious what the results would show. After a horrible day yesterday with the worst PET scan I have ever had I wasn't too sure. Lisa and I have been cautiously hopeful all week.

Then there was this morning. Seeing the doctor. Of course the nurses have no idea about your scan, or the PA's, so the buildup to seeing the doctor is somewhat maddening (much like this blog post!?). He (the doctor) came striding into the room with a big grin on his face and he said, "This is the best result I could have hoped for. Your tumors have reduced metabolic activity 30-40 percent and on top of that the tumors have shrunk about the same amount!" Not just less metabolic activity, but the tumor size has gone down. This is 100 percent unseen before in my body. Typically I'll see a drop in metabolic activity and then generally some tumor shrinkage. To see both, in less than a month, is nothing short of a miracle.

FRIDAY, JANUARY 11, 2013

Zero Time

I WAS GIVEN A SEVENTEEN PERCENT chance to live five years in 2007. This is my first "Zero Time" or "Negative Time" birthday. 30+1. Not only am I celebrating a further distance from the time they gave me to live, I am celebrating the news I got yesterday.

I imagine if someone was to ask me if I was surprised by the results yesterday I think I would say yes. Though I didn't consider them outside the realm of possibility to be sure. There have been times in the past where I went in feeling pretty good and hopeful just to have all that crushed (several times in fact...). So while we ask God for something like tumor death, it doesn't always happen and so we have to go into see the doctor a little guarded. Hopeful, but trying to find hope in God in that no matter WHAT the outcome of the scan or appointment that our hope rests firmly in God (all else will disappoint).

This time with all the prayers for healing in our life recently we had an expectation that we were going to see something different (for me, honestly, seeing the tumors grow would have been a sign to me that my death from this was assured and to get things in order...). Seeing the dramatic results though of tumor shrinkage was in many ways God reaching out to me and saying, "See, no one knows the time of their death but me. The trust they have in medical technology is nothing compared to what I can do."

Either way I learn something about God and myself. My faith grows.

FEBRUARY, HOUSTON

SATURDAY, FEBRUARY 2, 2013

Sooo, where are we at?

I FEEL LIKE A LOT OF MY life involves some kind of waiting. Six years ago waiting to see a doctor or, frankly, anything was difficult. Thirty minutes before a movie could seem like forever. While I illustrate to you how much time we spend waiting it's more to give you an idea of what my experience is like, I don't want to come across as complaining (though I think I am).

I have learned a lot about waiting, silence, and being "alone with my thoughts". I really enjoy being able to be quiet and spend time with my thoughts. It's hard to get "silence" per se, here in Houston, especially in the hospital. There is always someone in the hall talking too loudly about issues you wish you didn't know about the stranger, or "soothing" music is playing somewhere, or the AC vent is rattling, or the sirens in the street are blaring. It's noise I have almost come to ignore, and when I get to places like Colorado Springs, where there isn't as much ambient noise, I really feel like I can breathe. It feels like I have been holding my breath and finally I can breathe again. I am sure there is some quote somewhere about silence being a balm to the spirit or soul or something. I am coming to understand that.

MARCH, HOUSTON and SEATTLE

WEDNESDAY, MARCH 6, 2013

Maybe this is God telling me something

WELL, I HAVE PNEUMONIA AGAIN. Time to break out the horse pills... But it's better than the liquid that tastes like rocket fuel.

How are those tumors doing? They haven't changed since the last scan size wise. But the metabolic activity has increased, which means they are getting ready to grow. I am off the expensive chemo pills and they are connecting me up with the trial doctor, again, to see if there is anything he has up his sleeves.

I have never felt like God was telling me to

pursue different options, or look at other things that might kill cancer, or to stop taking medication at all. But looking at the order of events this last time really has me wondering if perhaps God isn't trying to tell me something. The scan previous to this one was after I had been prayed over several times and I had only been on the drug, really on it, for about two weeks (a week and a half maybe?) the reaction we saw could HARDLY be credited to the drug. It had barely hit my system at that point, and to do that much damage?

I wonder if the drug never had done anything. Maybe it was the prayer in the first place. What if that is the blessing that God has had for me? I don't know, but at this point I am confused because of things I thought I knew or things I had hoped for. I wish I had a more solid answer on this, or at least some sort of feeling or conviction. I feel like I am groping in the dark trying to find out what God wants me to do in relation to this thing that is quite literally my life, and I am not coming up with any answers.

I'm really tired, four years is a long time to be waiting for something. My only hope is in Christ, yet I don't feel like I have any answers in regard to THIS problem. Maybe I need to listen better.

THURSDAY, MARCH 7, 2013

Wonder and Welcome

I STARTED IN ON **G.K.** Chesterton's book, "Orthodoxy" this morning after hearing John Piper say that it is among the handful of books he has read more than once. While making my way through the introduction he makes this statement, "What could be more delightful than to have in the same few minutes all the fascinating terrors of going abroad combined with all the humane security of coming home again?"

While this comment was aimed more at the things that motivate us as humans, I wonder if it's not in essence what Heaven will be. Both the "fantastical terror" of the unknown and yet a sense of coming home after a long trip. Of finally arriving. It is something I think we all crave, adventure, finding new things, to go where people haven't been and return home to tell of our adventures.

Perhaps heaven is at once an adventure and a return home.

SUNDAY, MARCH 10, 2013

Getting ahead of myself

MY LAST POST ON THE STATE of my health also brought up that I was kind of confused about what God wanted from Lisa and I through this sickness. In my disappointment at an outcome I was expecting, I felt like something I wanted was perhaps the same thing as what God wanted. I don't know that isn't the case, but right now the timing isn't right. I, again, lost sight of an important fact; this isn't about me. The things I go through now aren't about me. If I draw more attention to myself than to God, then something isn't right. God can use this pain and suffering for His glory and benefit, but when I take that upon myself and use it to highlight ME then it's pointless.

You can get far, far ahead of me by considering the "gains" of this world a loss and looking at things like suffering and hardship as the benefit that they are to your relationship with Christ and the reward of Heaven. I still struggle with this. I ask for my life because I do not want to suffer. Almost anything in comparison to what I am going through now (in my mind at least) seems like it would be easy.

In the same regards, the present suffering is nothing compared to the glory of God in Heaven (Romans 8:18). It's easy to forget when I rely so much upon my eyes to convey "reality" to me. The "reality" conveyed to me through my eyes though is all part of this body and world which are fading and temporary. I need to stop relying on the ups and downs of my health to reflect the REAL reality of the things God wants me to be, to pursue, and to reflect while I am still alive.

The end of what is available to me medically to pursue the death of this disease in my body can be viewed as scary, intimidating, or even terrifying. In a lot of ways I have been grasping tightly to that handrail of medical technology. I can't say how my life would have been different if I had not pursued medical attention. It might have been shorter, it might not have been. But here, at the end of possibilities when science and the world around me say, "There is no chance" is a very great place for God to work.

I don't know that I am ready for death, or ever will be, no matter what age, but I have no doubt in my mind that God is there for me on the other side. When the things I could not view in this life, that are in fact "reality," become visible to me. I no longer fear what God has for me in the future. Be it health or a slow spiral into the breakdown of my body, as long as I am alive I know He still has something for me to do and reflect glory to Him. So... full steam ahead!

TUESDAY, MARCH 19, 2013

Feels like... pain

THE PAST WEEK I HAVE had something like three migraines. The most recent one was this morning and started about 9:30. I went to the hospital, got a blood draw, and then went upstairs to see the doctor about the drug trials.

As I was filling out paperwork I realized my vision was starting to disappear. It went from "being able to see" to "not being able to see" maybe the quickest I have ever had a migraine affect me. We rescheduled a new time to see the doc as I couldn't see a thing and was expecting my brain to explode in pain sometime soon. Lisa then lead me downstairs to the car and we made our way home where I took some meds and then spent a majority of the day in bed while my head threatened to separate itself from my body.

So we've rescheduled seeing the doctor for Wednesday afternoon. We'll see if there is anything he has suggestion wise for next steps in cancer fighting. My hope though really resides more in prayer and God's healing... because it doesn't destroy me in order to "make me better." I'm tired of being sick in order to be "healthy".

THURSDAY, MARCH 21, 2013

Goodbye MDA

I'VE THOUGHT OF HUNDREDS of ways to start this post. Funny, upbeat, a humorous anecdote, dark, depressing, full of words, a poem, or... who knows... none of them really seemed to work. I'm going to get right to the point. I saw two doctors at MDA today, both of them had no further options for me. The trial doctor had no further trials. My oncologist I've been seeing for the past three years, and some change, has no other options or things to try either. They still want to keep in touch, but the suggestion of my doctor was to start hospice as soon as possible. He has given me no more than six months to live. On average at this point in things he typically sees his patients last about two to three months.

I don't know what to say ("Oh, but you'll say it anyway." You're thinking...). I've been expecting this speech for about two and a half years now. Making it this far is nothing short of a miracle as it is. I've lived close to three times longer than the average patient with the same cancer. I kind of thought I would be freaking out when I got the news. Part of me is, I think... I don't know if you can really HELP but have some part of you just lose it when you get news like this (maybe I'm wrong?) but there is another part of me... a rather large part actually, that isn't freaking out. Generally today when I have cried it has been because other people come to mind and wondering how they will take this information rather than how I am dealing with it.

When I was first diagnosed with this I made the comment several times that sixteen percent chance to live five years was really narrow by the scientific definition, but was MORE than enough room for God to move. In fact the tighter the number, the smaller the chance, the greater the glory our Lord will receive when He does something amazing. And here I am... almost six years later, a year past that sixteen percent. Still alive and fighting (thank you Lord!).

And now there aren't any percentages. God knows when I will die, and how I will die. Be it two months from now, seven months from now, four years from now, or fifty years from now. The illusion is stripped away. There was always a one hundred percent chance I would die. If God chooses to use this cancer as the method for my transition to Heaven then that is the way of it.

BUT there is nothing keeping Him from claiming even more glory for Himself now by healing me from this cancer. When the potential for doubt about where the healing of my cancer came from is gone, there is nothing but glory to be given to God. Again, it's like the three guys in the book of Daniel thrown into the furnace. My furnace is getting horribly hot, but that doesn't change anything from God's perspective. Just because the doctors have no more medicines to try, no more tricks to pursue, or things to put into my body doesn't mean God stops working.

SATURDAY, MARCH 23, 2013

That was fast...

YESTERDAY WAS THE DAY I holed up and spent time with God and away from technology and food (I needed a TON of pain killer yesterday for some reason... though today I haven't touched it yet, and it's been over 12 hours since I had it last).

The big choice that came from yesterday was that we believe God is calling us back to Seattle. Between then and now though we plan on spending a few weeks in Colorado Springs, and then making an "epic" road trip to places in Colorado, Nevada, California, Oregon and Washington. We don't have any details about timelines or anything right now. I'll know more on Monday or Tuesday, but we will be packing up and moving fairly soon.

In other "God is working" categories I started writing this post and halfway through I got a ping on Facebook and a John and Naomi, friends of ours (who I look up to in many ways) have a potential living situation for Lisa and I, very cheaply, in the city of Bellevue... Before I even said anything about our move, God was on it. It fits just about everything we need, and it's really nice. I don't yet fully know if it's a go or not, but I had to share how God was supplying solutions before we even started down that road.

SUNDAY, MARCH 24, 2013

Too FAST

I GUESS THERE IS NO SUCH thing as outside of God's will... But I have to admit I think this might be faster than I anticipated.

Went to the ER this morning because I couldn't breathe after getting up and going to the bathroom. There they ran some tests and told me just about the last thing I wanted to hear: I have pneumonia in both lungs and the tumors are blocking airways on both sides.

They are keeping me in the hospital. I don't know what to say. If God is making this impossible to get out of to teach me something, it doesn't get much more impossible than this.

This is all coming down faster than anyone thought. I'm scared. I cry a lot, Lisa is crying a lot. The little man screaming in my head is overwhelming now. I am drowning. I need some major help. To be honest at this rate I might not make it beyond Wednesday.

Some hope restored

-by Lisa-

WHAT A DAY! THE FIRST DIAGNOSIS Ben got in the ER sounded incredibly bleak and caused us to think his life on Earth might be ending very soon.

But then later a palliative care doctor told him that most of his breathing problems were likely caused by the double pneumonia at this point, not the tumors, and that the pneumonia was very treatable through antibiotics. I think maybe his pneumonia three weeks ago just never went away and became further advanced. Additionally, the tumor growth could possibly be blocked by adding in a longer stent. There's definite plans to treat him and not just "make him comfortable."

We still don't know how events will turn, but were encouraged and overwhelmed in love with all the prayers and help we received today. From the chaplain who encouraged us, to so many texts, emails, Facebook notes, and phone calls, to the friends who visited us and brought us food today and will continue to visit, to all of you who lifted Ben and me up to God. God continues to write Ben's story and you're all a part of it.

When I left Ben, he was feeling a lot better: able to breathe enough oxygen, relaxed, and encouraged.

WEDNESDAY, MARCH 27, 2013

My head is spinning with activity!

THE PLAN AT THE MOMENT is to fly Lisa and I to Seattle on Saturday via the airlines with the proper tools at hand for me.

This is happening so very fast. They told me yesterday that if Seattle is where I wanted to be for hospice then I needed to leave ASAP as this is a window for me to get there. So ASAP we are leaving. Lisa has been packing up the apartment the past few days and we have plans to get a moving company to pick it all up and move it to

Seattle sometime after we leave. I have no idea what we need to do when it comes to closing down the apartment, but as we are looking at breaking the lease it looks like it's going to cost us an extra two months' rent.

I am doing better when it comes to shortness of breath. They have been giving me a painkiller/shortness of breath drug, plus a steroid that helps as well. I am also on oxygen (which either doesn't stay on at night or makes my nose bleed because it's so far in my nose with all the dry air) which seems to help a lot.

Also my hair is starting to turn brown again... Mixed in under the blonde. It's going to look interesting here in a few weeks.

Fear and stress wise things have been lessoning a bit. It tends to be the worse in the morning and then gets better during the day, and then it seems to carry over from the previous day if I had a good day (like I did yesterday). Yesterday I had a good day. I had Ryan, a friend, visit me at lunch and pray for me, and we talked a bit, it was really nice for him to spend his lunch visiting. Then Greg, a friend of mine from a few hours away, heard we might be leaving before he could see us so he left work, drove the couple of hours and hung out with me in the evening. Then we had dinner and had a bit of a tearful goodbye (just moving to Seattle is hard enough as he is close enough to see me every so often).

God moved in another way yesterday evening

as well! My mom got a call from Dr. Leland Teng, a guy in Seattle who wants to be my doctor! He goes to the church my parents used to go to and Lisa's parents know him as well. I guess he is kind of hard to get an appointment with because he dedicates his time to more charity based work cases... Like mine might be. He called out of the blue and was asking questions about me and when I heard about it I was like "Yes!" So something I was slightly concerned about, having a doctor there in Seattle and available "on the ground" when I get there was very important to me. Plus he has had experience with cancer and hospice before. Another God thing was that I had two different, unsolicited people recommend the same hospice to me yesterday via email. Then the Case Manager had pulled a few names from the Internet of potential Hospice options and that one was one of them. I think we'll be going with that one.

THURSDAY, MARCH 28, 2013

Never know who's watching you

I WAS TOLD AT THE ONSET of this cancer that I was being forced into the spotlight and I would never really know how many people would be watching, observing, criticizing, praying, and/or learning from what I do, how I react to things, or my general attitude in response to everything that comes my way. Up until this week I really had NO idea what kind of effect I had been having amongst the staff at MDA. The staff at MDA rarely talk about themselves or their reaction to things.

This week I have been flooded with comments from staff, both that I have known a while (who have come to visit me) and staff I have worked with just this week alone. I have been blown away what a little bit of a good attitude, faith in Christ, and an upbeat personality has had effect wise on the doctors, and other staff here in the hospital.

Word seems to have gotten around and I have spent a lot of extra time talking to people that would normally blow in and blow out of the room. The point of this isn't to paint a picture of how great God has made me (because I am not great) but to point out that if God is working in your life it is going to be IMPOSSIBLE to know what kind of effect He is going to have in your life amongst those around you who aren't, or maybe even those that ARE, Christians in your life.

Knowing this, knowing that God has given me the ability to have a somewhat positive outlook on what is happening to me, and being able to share that with the staff here has really been a great way to show Jesus in my life to the staff here. Just as you are getting my story through this blog, they have been getting my story through serving me and talking to me here in the hospital.

I learned earlier this week that of all the people the social worker sees that my attitude and outlook put me in the top two percent of patients he sees.

Before he left today he wished we had had more time to spend together. The fellow/doctor who has been in charge of my case isn't a Christian, and in fact he said he doesn't really go in for religious stuff, but that studies have shown that those people with "religion" do much better at these kinds of settings than other people… I think until he met me that was just a study in his mind… He's spent a lot of time talking to me about faith. And then a nurse I have had was blown away by the fact that I could make jokes and laugh despite what was happening. Then a long term nurse friend of mine from downstairs came up to say goodbye as well and she informed me that my outlook and faith have really inspired her and it had been a pleasure to work with me.

Overall it is nice to know God is using me despite the greater issues I am going through, and learning a long time ago that worrying won't add one more day or hour to my lifespan really helped me to cling to God and thus turn the mirror of my life to reflecting Him. This isn't meant to be a pat on the back to say what a great job I am doing, but an encouragement to you to live your life reflecting Jesus Christ and your faith in him. You never know who is keeping an eye on you, or what they might get from your life.

FRIDAY, MARCH 29, 2013

The net and the wire

BEING SICK ENOUGH TO GO TO the hospital can be like walking on a tightrope. It's about balance in your life, with or without a big balancing pole. When you're in the hospital it's like working with a net under you... Even if it's not true. The net gives you some idea that if you fall you're going to be caught and NOT break your neck and die. So you learn to work with the wire and the net. Then they eventually release you to try it on your own. Generally I do just fine. I am often kind of grumpy the first day back from the hospital and others suffer for my insecurities, but it evens out and I get on with life.

The problem here is that I have come to the realization that the net the hospital seems to put under you in times of trouble is in fact one made of flimsy cheap rope. That if you fall in the hospital, off the rope and plummet to the ground, you are just as dead. It might happen more slowly, but you're going to reach the bottom with enough force to kill you eventually. The irony here is that the real net is Jesus Christ. He's the net we can't see, and when it's our time to get off the rope we will fall, but HE is there to catch us at the bottom. And if we really trust him with our lives then the fall at the end of the wire work looks spectacular and gives praise to God for training such magnificent wire workers in their dismounts.

I have been struggling with my potential dismount. I feel like part of this past week was dismount training. Maybe a little bit of "how to fall" training. Leaving the hospital today the realization that the fake net I had come to put a little bit of reliance on was gone hit me hard... About the same time I had some trouble breathing. It's scary trying to balance this sickness on the wire so high off the ground with everyone watching. What kind of dismount will I have? How will the end of that show glorify God? Is this the end of the act? Or do I get to reach the end and turn around and start a new act?

Either way I need peace about it. It's scary being up here with lots of eyes on you. Breathing alone is hard enough these days.

SUNDAY, MARCH 31, 2013

To land amidst the trees

WE MADE IT TO SEATTLE. Yesterday was a pretty big blur in my mind. Between some final packing moments by some great friends who sacrificed some of their precious time to come down from Dallas to put our apartment in boxes, going to the airport, feeling like I was holding my breath through most of the airport, and then being on the flight, and then getting off the flight, making it to Lisa's parents' house, and waking up this morning, it seems like a huge big blur.

But there we are. I've awoken on Resurrection Sunday, among the trees of Lisa's family's house. Still alive a week after some doctors in the ER said that I probably wouldn't make it this long. God has brought friends and family together to be there to encourage me to bring me to where I am now. I would say this last week that I could have made some new friends, but don't know if I will ever have time to cultivate those... Perhaps my just being there and them seeing what I was and what God was doing was enough. God used me to touch them, and it is my hope that that touch goes far beyond this week, instilling life and hope in their lives, much like God showed them in mine. Never have I felt so purposeful being in a hospital room.

The flight yesterday was interesting. We had first class tickets and also a couple hundred things that could have gone wrong. Despite everything that COULD have gone wrong I can only think of a handful of slightly grumpy people that could have had a better attitude, but other than that, it went fairly flawlessly. The only "strange" thing was the battery pack in the air compressor I carried with me was supposed to last five hours. Subtract "promises" and I expected perhaps a good 3 hours out of it. The flight was four hours and twelve minutes. Maybe an hour and a half into the flight my battery pack decided it was going to die. We had to go through the hassle of switching the battery between two plane seats (this device is the size of a carry-on suitcase). Got it replaced and turned down the airflow even more to 1 liter of oxygen extra an hour. Figured that would save me. So between dinner and a movie and napping three hours rolls around and guess what? I have almost no battery life left. I had to be very delicate until we got to the car so I could plug it in. Oh well. God got me through it all and here I am this morning. Despite the hiccups, the transitions, the things that could have gone wrong, and the things that went flawlessly, God was there and He helped us get here.

I am tired, yesterday was rough, but I woke up this morning with the oxygen off my face and I got up and went to the bathroom without needing to use it. I think I am getting better at pacing myself (it beats dragging this noisy monster around with me...) but seriously, I'll do what I need to do God's will for me.

APRIL, SEATTLE

MONDAY, APRIL 1, 2013

Here's to Houston

DEAR TEXAS, HOUSTON SPECIFICALLY,

I cannot begin to describe to you how you have affected our lives. When we first started heading south to see your highly trained medical staff, there was very little we liked about you. Sure the food options were impressive, and the people started to open up a little to us, but the heat, traffic, LONG wait times to see a doc for 10 minutes, and confusing torn up streets really didn't do a lot to win us over.

Fast forward to almost three years later and we have learned a lot. The road issues haven't changed, though frankly some of your quirks (feeder/

frontage roads? Brilliant!) we have grown fond of. The food situation we will miss. I don't know anywhere we have lived where the food has been as good as it is in Houston. So many options (even, after years of looking, Asian...) and so many colors.

The most important thing we will miss about you Texas, Houston specifically, are your people. (When you aren't in your cars...) Your hospitality, your generosity, your openness... They are ALL things that Lisa and I have learned a lot from. You welcomed us into your lives so quickly when we first went down there and instantly started providing food and prayer for us. You filled our freezer and our hearts with your love.

Then once we got settled down a bit we started to learn from you about what it is to make friends and get to know each other better. Bible studies, conversations over board games, lunch after church, outings, guys nights, girls nights, solo dinners together, discussions about the deep and potentially unknowable depths of God, and BBQ. Because of these we DID get to know you better, and in getting to know you better we opened up to you and you got to know US better, which lead to your deep generosity.

You can say that you have learned things from me and my journey, but you have taught me and Lisa a thing or two about what it means to open up to people on our own and be welcoming. These are things we will hold dear to our hearts and hopefully make us more welcoming Christians who can bless others as we have been so richly blessed.

You have touched us Houston, and despite the things we have said about disliking you, you have left an indelible mark on our lives...one that will not soon wear off, and I think to some degree I had hoped would go on for a few years longer. Having it "cut short" at this point in the game honestly makes me feel like we have some unfinished business that needs resolving. I don't know if God will bring us back to you at some point, or if this is it for this life for us, but you need to know that you have made your mark on our lives and we will miss you. From your food to your depth of character, to the laughs, to a deeper understanding of what hospitality actually is.

Thank you, thank you, and thank you.

WEDNESDAY, APRIL 3, 2013

Colorado, my Heart

COLORADO IS WHERE WE FEEL our hearts called to. We both have companies there and absolutely love our jobs. I cannot think of a job I would like more than the one I have when I can do it full time. Lisa's job is not only a continual challenge to her, but her employers have become great friends and they care deeply for us. Both of our companies really have adopted us in some form or another as family of the members of the company. Holidays with them, plenty of food, even staying for weeks at a time while up from Houston. They accepted us, and we happily accepted and became a part of their lives as much as they became a part of ours.

The passion I have to do what I have been doing in Colorado Springs and what I want to be doing there is hot and bright, and aside from the pain of the tumors and the shortness of breath nothing "bothers" me more on a daily basis. My mind has such great ideas and hopes for things that God has put in my head to try and improve missions with technology and helping "ordinary" people get involved with what God is doing around the world. (I can talk about that a lot and love brainstorming on the topic)

We made some close friends in Colorado Springs, but by the very nature of the city (very transient) a lot of our friends themselves moved on to other places in the world where God called them to be. (Thailand, San Antonio, Seattle, Mexico, Spain, African states, the Middle East, and China come to mind) While our hearts are in Colorado Springs and what we have been involved in there, a lot of the people who love and care for us have followed God's call to other places... which is ultimately the true goal of the thing that brings passion to what I do.

While we consider Colorado a place we hope to return to should the Lord heal me, it wasn't really in the "running" for us to land for this point in our lives. Colorado Springs is representative of a hope of what can be done and what still needs to be done. It's about potential and promises fulfilled. I might get to be a part of that, and then I might not get to join in that. The call is entirely my Lord and Father's. I am His to do with as He desires. He knows where I want to be and what I want to be doing, I've told Him... I've asked you to tell Him, and we've all prayed for it. So if that isn't what happens, then God has something far better in it for all of us, as disappointing as that might seem to us right now.

The support from Colorado Springs, and the desire to have us back there is great, and we thank all of you for that. I want you to know that it's our hope to go back. In reflecting on this, God's leading and directions seem that much more focused. The way He's opened doors for us. Laid open details before we asked for them, and set the light before our paths before we even thought to ignite the lamp. He's truly a great and amazing God. He brought us safe thus far, and I have faith that no matter what happens between us and this cancer, that He will use it to impact everyone who knows about it, and everyone who will hear about it.

Thank you Colorado Springs, OC International, Pulpit Rock Church, and LGA Studios, for being a part of it all, and for being an embodiment of hope for us. It doesn't mean that it'll happen, but for us Colorado is still out there, and God's promises are renewed every morning, so, maybe someday again, and soon.

FRIDAY, APRIL 5, 2013

Facebook Update

BIBLE GATEWAY WITH A THOUGHT on bearing the cross of Christ, even if just for a tiny bit. It encouraged me this morning.

"And remember, though Simon had to bear the cross for a very little while, it gave him lasting honour. Even so the cross we carry is only for a little while at most, and then we shall receive the crown, the glory. Surely we should love the cross, and, instead of shrinking from it, count it very dear, when it works out for us 'a far more exceeding and eternal weight of glory.'"

— Charles Spurgeon

Facebook Update

I WOKE UP WITH A RATHER HIGH anxiety... My body claimed it was having a hard time getting air, I think it was fine. Took some anti anxiety meds anyway. Tried listening to some music in order to calm down. Nothing was helping. Suddenly the rain picks up and I get a beautiful orchestra of drips, drops, puddles, flows, sloshes, pats, skitters, and a general merry melody of the pre-dawn gentle rain. God has blessed me with a means of dozing off to sleep despite my best efforts of man-made music could provide. Thank you Father for, again, answering my prayers before I even had them. And now, to sleep.

TUESDAY, APRIL 9, 2013

PR4913

The title of this post is shorthand for Prayer Request 4/9/13.

PART OF HOSPICE AS WELL is being honest with the patient. This morning the nurse was being frank with me, and it was hard. The scientific folks, those with records to my charts and whatnot, don't seem to have a lot of hope left for me for much of anything. It's hard because they want to be "honest" and not sugar coat anything ("You're doing fine! Go outside and run around like you're six!") when something like that might kill me. It's hard. I'm not sure where the line needs to be.

Sleep/ dreams: Every time I mention this I am amazed. I am very much starting to realize the unconscious mind/sleeping mind is more susceptible to things spiritual than the awake mind might be led to believe. When I ask for help with protection against bad, scary, horrific, lingering, or harmful dreams, I do not get bad dreams. Period. I can see that as nothing BUT an answer to prayer. My dreams and the things that run through my head are so much safer when I am being prayed for, which leads to much better sleep, which leads to being more awake during the day, which leads to having better days.

Hope: I continue to hope greatly... extravagantly in fact. I know where God is going to take me in all this so I have hope that it'll be different from anywhere or any way perhaps "science" might be able to explain (and as so much of our society is built on what "science" says, I am hoping that WE all might learn something bigger about God through this whole process. My hope remains in Christ, which leads me to a different place than if I was just staring down death on my own).

My shortness of breath: I continue to lose ground on the blood oxygen level. This morning, while I felt like I was doing well (forcing myself to move like a turtle) my oxygen level stayed in the mid to upper 80's. This was when my nurse informed me that it would probably continue to decrease from here on out. My heart is also working extra hard to compensate for that as well.

On April 12th, Ben went to the hospital for a procedure that might have been able to relieve the pressure in his lungs and make it easier for him to breathe. It turned out that he didn't have the problem that would have warranted this solution, so the procedure wouldn't have helped and wasn't performed.

SUNDAY, APRIL 14, 2013

Concedure

HOPE IS A LOT LIKE GLASS. I would say it rarely forms in the wild the same way as it does in captivity, even if it does get hot enough. The point being the hope is delicate. It's a fragile thing that can be up-ended on the sidewalk with barely a second glance. Trip. Poof. Shatter. Gone.

Last week I got a call about a procedure they wanted to do in hopes of opening up my lung capacity. It involved the fact that I had ballooned some almost ten pounds in a short amount of time due to liquid weight. They had me run all over the hospital and then settled me into a room where they slapped hot goo on my back, did the ultrasound thing for a few minutes and then cleaned me off. "There is no liquid" came the verdict. "There is nothing we can do."

They sent me home. Not a grand scheme of things by way of verdicts, but it was a hope building exercise. "This might hurt, but it'll help you breathe better at the end of it." That wasn't to be the case. I am kind of running at the bottom of supposedly medical technology (or at least half-hearted types). I am discouraged by the medical attempts and in the future I might just say no to them.

Last evening Thomas Hallstrom and his wife Kate visited us and they just happened to be part of a band (Hallstrom) that we really enjoy (my top 25 iTunes list is populated with their music). I hadn't met Kate before so we got to hang out and chat and then they sang a few songs for us, and it was really touching. It's been a long time since I have heard live music and it was a blessing to me. If any of you want to come and play live music I am okay with it.

Making it upstairs took something like fifty minutes and then another handful of time to get to bed. The source of the problem seems to be anxiety/ stress/ panic attack. I get to a place where I draw a single breath wrong and it "snowballs" into this pattern of incorrect breathing that I can't control, and then I start freaking out. Be it either hyperventilating (I think I was doing this last night) or not getting enough breath (which I tend to do by default) I start to get scared and generally Lisa will have to come in and put her arm around me and I breathe a certain way to synchronize my breathing to hers. It's a sticky downward spiral that I cannot control.

THURSDAY, APRIL 18, 2013

Looking for Whole Healing

I **HAVE BEEN READING THROUGH** the book, "Glorious Ruin," albeit casually, and I have been stumbling upon goldmine after goldmine of things to think about. The other night I was sitting and talking with my good friend Ryan about being very confused about God giving me all sorts of abilities and talents and then seemingly taking them away from me prematurely. "Why did God give me so much passion? So much desire? So much kick, so much fight, when He was going to take it away so soon? I mean there are hundreds of people, THOUSANDS of people who don't care about life, who casually they throw it away, or go through life with a ho-hum attitude. Meanwhile, here I am fighting cancer and trying to work a job that I love and have a passion for."

I don't understand it. And before you take to telling me that life isn't fair (thanks, I got that one already) I guess when I talk to God I generally do it one on one and not in a general, "Why me?" Yesterday after Ryan left, the author of the book I was reading quoted a counselor of his (Larry Crabb). He said, "If you don't go to your grave confused, you don't go to your grave trusting."

Boom. Like a hammer to a plate glass window. I would say that my troubles boil down to trust in God. Trusting that He is doing what He is doing in my life. However I don't see many troubles in my life at this point. God has brought me around to this place and blessed me here in Seattle. My "troubles" are simply thing that don't matter when lined up against other things that DO matter (or essentially, my "troubles" are life vs. death, pure and simple).

I love my job. I love my life. I love my wife. But sometimes the blessings I have been given do not make sense to me when it comes to dying at this age. But that comes down to trust then it doesn't matter at what age I go, because God knows what He is doing. It's like asking for more work when you've been called in for rest hours ago. I might not understand it, but I have to trust it.

Then there is the flip side, while I hold my breath (ummm, no pun intended right now) and ask God to heal me. To bring me around to being made whole again. I don't think there is anything wrong with trusting God and asking to be healed. I think until my last breath I will be asking to be healed. I ask because I see benefit in it. God has given me a vision to see where things are going and an excitement to get them there. If He heals me then I would love to help tackle that problem with my whole heart. But if He doesn't then I have to trust that He is keeping His kingdom together and keeping it in line and I get to rest, while others get to toil. It comes down to trust.

BUT there is something on top of that that you need to be aware of: I'm not dead yet. It seems the more I live the more people tend to put me in my grave. I encounter this more and more. Mourn me when I am dead, rejoice with me as living while I am alive. If God chooses to heal me then I will have years ahead of me... Putting me in my grave now just makes everyone sadder than they need to be. It might be "obvious" to you which way God is going, but you don't know when, how, or why, so please don't go putting me in that place until I have taken that last breath. There is hope until then, and there is trust in God until then.

THURSDAY, APRIL 25, 2013

Swinging low

TODAY WAS ONE OF THOSE days where I never really fell asleep. I was super tired from last night and never really was able to get the sleep I was looking for. Or the sleep I was craving. A lot of dreams that were really strange, but nothing that ever took shape, and in fact I could feel them linger on me for a long time. Kind of like some nervous energy that never really found a home. Some of it I wonder if it has to do with my disease? I mean most of the time, people say I am doing really well (doctors, other folks, etc.) with handling the fact that people say that I am dying. Then there are other times where it seems like I can't seem to get air. Sometimes I wonder, you know? God could totally shore this up and it would be just fine and then I wonder if that is just overreaching optimism.

Today I am tired. Deep down, I wish I knew for sure which way this would go. Today is a pessimistic day I think. I canceled two appointments because I had a migraine, and now I am sitting here with nothing but sweat and bad feelings.

SUNDAY, APRIL 28, 2013

Facebook Update

MADE IT TO CHURCH FOR A LITTLE BIT. It was good to see everyone we did. Thank you all.

MAY, SEATTLE

SUNDAY, MAY 5, 2013

Facebook Update

BREATH IS COMING HARD TONIGHT could use prayers.

In early May, Ben and Lisa headed to Lake Crescent for a weekend of relaxation, prayer, and time to reconnect. Lake Crescent, in the Olympic National Forest, was Ben's favorite place.

WEDNESDAY, MAY 8, 2013

Lake Crescent

~by Lisa~

THE COUPLE OF DAYS AWAY at Lake Crescent Lodge were really fantastic. Gorgeous weather in an amazing place, and we were able to get out and enjoy it! Plus have some prayer time and conversations with each other that haven't fit into our hectic and tiring lives of late. Our souls and relationship were greatly restored. There were no emergency calls to hospice for Ben, just a couple of necessary naps.

On the way back we spent a couple hours with Ben's brother and sister-in-law in Tacoma. Then on Sunday, a ~~band of angels~~ worship band from Capitol Hill came to play for us and about 25 visitors. My sister recruited them without having heard them play (she's good friends with one of the players), so we were fortunate that they were talented musicians with a great repertoire and a desire to praise God for his salvation.

But all of the excitement took its toll, because for the past couple days Ben has been wiped out. He's having more trouble breathing, little appetite, more pain, and a lack of focus (though that's largely because of how doped up he is). I'm encouraged that today was significantly better than yesterday, and that his nurse agrees with me that the big increase in problems is mostly because of how much activity he had for four days. So, a quiet life for now. It's a good thing we're used to being at home a lot.

THURSDAY, MAY 9, 2013

The End (and a new Beginning)

-by Lisa-

BEN PASSED AWAY AT 2:30AM on May 9th. He died peacefully at the hospital. I already miss him terribly, but am so glad that he isn't hurting and suffering anymore, and even more that he is with Jesus now - "to live is Christ, to die is gain."

Starting Sunday night, breathing became extremely hard for Ben, even with all the help we could give him at home. He seemed to improve on Tuesday - and I thought that he would stabilize for a time. But on Wednesday morning his doctor said "You don't have long left now," and he was right. The difficulty breathing began to make Ben anxious, and he started to act somewhat irrationally - trying to pull off his breathing mask and get up to walk around.

As his distress increased, I read Psalms to him, including some of his favorites, Psalm 20 and 40. At one point a verse said "God is our rescue," and Ben looked directly at me in a moment of clarity and coherence and said "I need to be rescued!" It was then I called the hospice center again, and this led to Ben's admission to Overlake Hospital.

At the hospital, Ben (if he had been more aware) would have been so impressed with the team we had. Both an exceptional ER doctor and Inpatient doctor, who were very present, positively communicative, and interested in giving Ben the treatment he wished. As a hospital visitor veteran, I can say that I knew Ben was so well-cared for, as were my parents and I as we stayed with Ben.

I knew from conversations we had previously that Ben didn't want any invasive measures taken to prolong his life, and just to be as free of pain and anxiety as possible. In his stage of disease, artificial respiration and such doesn't save lives, but mostly causes discomfort to the patient while possibly prolonging their life for just a short time. The doctors helped Ben to lay quietly, sedated enough that his failing breath from his fluid-filled lungs didn't distress him. My parents and I stood over Ben for his hours in the hospital, praying over him and singing hymns about our hope in Christ. I hope that as he heard us, he was encouraged in his final hours.

I'm so grateful that we had a special time together at Lake Crescent; and that he got to see so many people who were important to him this week and in the past few weeks in Seattle.

Ben is done with his broken body and now has a new, amazing one. He is with the One who loves Him more than anything and saved his soul. And I personally believe that Ben's adventures have only just begun. I look forward to celebrating with him someday!

POSTLUDE

SATURDAY, OCTOBER 8, 2011

The inevitability of endings

This post, written by Ben on October 8, 2011, makes a fitting end to this story.

ENDINGS. EVERYTHING FROM TIME spent on the beach, a good book, a great meal, a noteworthy career, or as simple as the candy in the candy bowl. Some of them are replenishable, easily replaced, and others are difficult to match, and never truly forgotten.

This has been an amazing week. I've gotten to see, hang out with, and talk with some family members I haven't gotten to do that with in a very long time. (Something, perhaps, I did not know I was missing until I experienced it.) Here we are at the almost end of it, with medical tests, pokings, and drugs looming just over the next rise and my desire to replay these past two weekends is very strong.

I am tired from late nights, health issues, and a lot of extra time spent with people, but this past week was a great week and one I hope we can duplicate again, and often, this side of Heaven. I have to confess that I think perhaps my schedule and treatments made me focus a little more on myself, and in focusing on getting better I forgot about things like family as I strove to find a cure for my ailments. The benefits I have had emotionally this week rival that of any healing skill MDA has leveled at me these past few years.

That is probably the hardest and most convicting paragraph I have written in a very long time.

I've learned a lot this weekend and I don't think it's an accident that it happened while I was away from the "normal" things of my strange life.

It's at times like these when I am faced with such a big reminder to how different things could have been or how they could be so drastically different from the way they are now, that I find myself thinking about Heaven. I've been thinking a bit lately about different views of the afterlife and how, for some reason, the one that is prevalent in our culture, really almost despite your Faith and what it tells you, is that whatever happens after life is boring.

I just spent an amazing week with family where we didn't really have anything to do other than enjoy the weather, eat, hang out with each other, and go exploring. How is that not a model for how Heaven will be? God created us for life, and so I would assume that Heaven, as a reward for life, would have to be amazing. Just like a week of vacation is a reward for a year of hard work. Or like a great retirement, you now have the tools and the resources to do amazing things.

I don't think Heaven is going to be boring, I think it'll be the time when we have the resources to do some things we never had time to do here on Earth, and it'll be in a completely different way than we could have done it here. It's not a fully fleshed out thought, but the more I think about it the more I don't buy into boring at all.

But it takes a pretty drastic ending to get there. Perhaps that is the point of all the little endings in life... To prepare us for bigger endings. But you know it's not JUST about the endings. As we face an ending we also are faced with beginnings and we also need to know how to handle those just as effectively as we face a good farewell party.

Thanks team.

ALTAR CALL

EVERYONE WHO HAS CHRIST as savior is forgiven through his sacrifice, and will be with Him and with Ben when we all die. God's gift to us, if we believe in Him and receive Him into our lives, is this eternal life. I hope that anyone who wants to know more about this will talk to someone who knows Jesus.

APPENDIX

SUNDAY, JANUARY 1, 2010

How to Help 101

-by Lisa-

BECAUSE OF OUR SITUATION THESE suggestions are directed more at illness, but they could be adapted to other difficult conditions as well.

1. Don't give up

At first onset, it's easier to enthusiastically support someone who is hurting. But when the problem doesn't go away, what then? Is God not listening to your prayers? Is the sufferer lacking in faith? What do you say to them? Most greeting cards say "Get well soon!" not "Stick it out!"

Take heart, there are many righteous people who suffer indefinitely on this earth even with the prayers of others. In these cases God is glorified by the sufferer's faith and by the perseverance of those around them, not by a miraculous healing (although we hope!).

2. Be specific

We received many well-meaning offers of "Let me know if you need anything!" But what is "anything?" It is much more helpful to tell someone "I can watch your children for 4 hours this week," "Let me know how I can sign up to bring a meal/give you a ride," or "I'd love to clean your bathroom! When can I do that?"

Some of our best encouragement came from creative people who really thought about what we might need. Remember that the person you are trying to help is possibly too overwhelmed to give assignments and also that it is very humbling to ask for help in our culture.

3. Be silent, but don't disappear

Many are worried about what to say to a sufferer. Really, your presence says much more than words ever could! Please, please don't let awkwardness keep you from showing support. Your friend/family member is probably not waiting for your words of wisdom, just your love. Also, it's difficult to go wrong with the Bible or "I'm praying for you".

4. Don't compare

Sometimes sufferers need to talk about their situation, other times they need distraction. Be open to either possibility. If someone going through a difficult time asks about your life, NEVER say "Well, I don't want to burden you with my problems..." They are asking because A) they want to think of something else and B) they care about you.

We have realized that all suffering is relative. Week after week of chemo becomes normal. What might be most difficult for you could be manageable for me – and vice versa. Just because my husband has cancer doesn't mean I think your problems are trivial. Suffering is not competitive!

TUESDAY, JUNE 22, 2010

Ten Tips to Avert the Risk of Falling

BEFORE WE STARTED OUR WAIT for the doctor this time around I was handed a pamphlet entitled, "*Patient Safety: A Guide to Preventing Falls*," in which there was a section entitled, "Top Ten Quick Tips to Reduce Your Risk of Falls in Outpatient Areas and at Home". (Seems to exclude public places like grocery stores) Being us (Lisa and I) as we sat there we started to come up with ten... alternative methods for avoiding falls. We thought we would share with you. So without further ado: "Ten Tips to Avert the Risk of Falling"

1. Don't Stand Up (IE: Don't get off the couch, or out of bed. Whirling Dervishes are out.)
2. Avoid Angry Reindeer (I'll explain this one sometime this week, suffice to say we both had tears in our eyes over this.)
3. Become Royalty (And be carried everywhere, no more being "pushed" around in a wheelchair, it's a palanquin for you everywhere you go.)
4. Use a jet pack (The compressed air type, jet fuel indoors can be... flammable.)
5. Call it Autumn (If you don't get it, wait for it...)
6. Ignore Gravity (You can't fall, if, well, you CAN'T fall.)
7. Don't Fall
8. Lay off the drugs (That make you dizzy)
9. Eat (Lack of food makes one dizzy)
10. Don't age past 50

These are, of course, all in jest, please don't take them seriously. (As much as possible) We also determined from the pamphlet that Lisa is a greater fall risk than I am.

Ben Morrell

MONDAY, NOVEMBER 7, 2011

Wear Sunscreen

THE TITLE REFERS TO A PARODY song done by "Three Dead Trolls in a Baggie." I felt the content of this blog post was a bunch of shotgun statements about some of the things I have learned in the past five years. I wrote this to a friend of ours who was diagnosed with cancer and so I took the time to put some of this together.

Nurses are your friends. They will look out for you (sometimes maybe too much).

You, your husband, or a close friend or family member who chooses to help, needs to be as aware as you are (because you might not be sometimes) about what your treatment should be. Every time they hook you up to something, inject something in you, radiate, or do surgery, confirm what they are doing. It might be written wrong on the orders. Just because a piece of paper says something, doesn't mean it's what the doctor told you. If that data conflicts, have them contact the doctor. Do not simply "go with it." Case in point: I went two rounds of chemo getting a thing that was supposed to protect my liver, however when it combines with the chemo before it's in my veins it has the possibility of making my intestines bleed. I have to make sure every time that they don't accidentally mix these two things before I get them.

Find something that helps you communicate

what you are going through. I write (maybe a no-duh statement there...) but maybe it's having friends who will listen to what you have to say in an honest manner. Keeping everything (questions, thoughts, answers) bottled up inside doesn't help. And there is bound to be a lot of everything these next few months.

Enjoy life. [Laugh] This is going to sound strange but, it's only cancer. Yes, it's terrifying when you sit down to think about it, but honestly, I've never found freaking out to help in my treatment at all. God has a plan for my life, just like yours no matter if you are freaking out, worried, anxious, sad, happy, joyful, etc. However, I do think that while your attitude doesn't affect God, it does affect the people around you and how they feel about God sometimes.

This is going to be hard to read I think, it was hard for me to hear when I first heard it years ago: You have been given a pretty special gift with your cancer. This is God calling you, and your husband, out of your lives and saying, "Hey, I want you to get to know me better. It won't be easy, but I'm here, and my Love is far deeper and wider than you can imagine right now. And this is the way you're going to learn about the depth of my love."

God will provide. Sometimes in strange ways. But something that Lisa and I had to learn was that we had to let go of some pride to allow people to help us. People helping you do things (cook, watch kids, drive to the hospital with you, clean the house, clean the bathroom, hang out with you, etc) is partially for you, but it's also for the person helping. It's a way that God can use your life to help someone else learn more about serving people who need it. And that ranges from the emotional to the physical. Let people serve you, be available to be helped, let people know how they can help. You'll learn some things and so will they.

Be careful of superstitions. Both about healing stuff, and spiritual stuff. "I drank 14 liters of carrot juice before the last MRI I had and the tumor was smaller, I need to do that again!" or, "God won't heal me if I don't read the Bible enough." Things that you KNOW if you think about it aren't true, but it's really easy to fall into that way of thinking.

People you don't know, barely know, or perhaps know well, will scour the Internet attempting to find cures for you. Smile and nod, 98% of that stuff is crazy talk. They are just trying to help, and some people cope with what you are going through in their own way by trying to help. Maybe you can redirect their energy to other things... like scrubbing toilets (if they really want to be helpful when searching through crap...)

God's not going anywhere. Asking "why" won't really solve anything either. There will be so many why's by the end of this trial, some you know and others you don't. Go with it, ask God for strength and wisdom, and dive in.

Hair - Ok, I understand that hair means different things to different people, but in my book getting well is more important than looking good. Remember your identity is in Christ, not in how you look that morning.

REFERENCES

August 23, 2007

Quote from the August 17 entry of C.H. Spurgeon's daily devotional, "Faith's Check Book."

October 2, 2007

Quote from "The Journals of Jim Elliot," page 278, September 24.

January 1, 2008

Quote from the last stanza of C.S. Lewis's poem, "Love's As Warm As Tears."

May 23, 2009

The blog post mentioned is from the blog, Stuff Christians Like, written by Jon Acuff May 22, 2009. Archives can be found here: http://www.jonacuff.com/stuffchristianslike/2009/05/i-dont-want-a-life-that-requires-much-faith/

March 19, 2012

Quote from Chuck Smith's Mark 2-3 C2000 Series on The Blue Letter Bible. Full commentary can be found here: http://www.blueletterbible.org/commentaries/comm_view.cfm?AuthorID=1&ContentID=7131&comminfo=25&topic=Mark.

July 28, 2012

A.W. Tozer quote mentioned by Ben is a colloquial version of this Tozer quote from Chapter 39 of "*Glorify His name! The root of the righteous*." The original quote is as follows: "It is doubtful whether God can bless a man greatly until He has hurt him deeply."

March 7, 2013

Quote from the Introduction of G.K. Chesterton's "Orthodoxy," which was published in 1908.

April 5, 2013

Quote from Bible Gateway's Facebook status from April 5, 2013. Post can be found here: https://www.facebook.com/BibleGateway/posts/10151520692792010

April 18, 2013

Quote from page 143 of Tullian Tchividjian's book, "Glorious Ruin: How Suffering Sets You Free."

Made in the USA
Lexington, KY
28 September 2017